Maurizio Martinelli Giulio Paolucci

ETRUSCAN
P L A C E S

SCALA

Contents

5 INTRODUCTION

25 THE MAJOR CENTERS
OF LAZIO

25 Caere (Cerveteri)
33 Pyrgi
34 Tarquinii (Tarquinia)
43 Gravisca (Porto Clementino)
44 Vulci
48 Cosa (Ansedonia)
50 The Production of *Bucchero*
52 Religion
54 The Museo Archeologico
Nazionale in Tarquinia
58 The Museo Nazionale
Etrusco di Villa Giulia

65 THE UPPER VALLEY
OF THE TIBER, VEII
AND LAKE BOLSENA

65 The Faliscan Region,
Capena and Lucus Feroniae
67 Falerii (Civita Castellana)
71 Sutri and Nepi
73 Veii (Veio)
75 Bisenzio
77 The Area around Volsinii
78 Volsinii (Orvieto)
84 Bolsena

86 Places of Worship
88 The Museo Archeologico
Nazionale in Orvieto
90 The Museo Archeologico
"Claudio Faina"

95 RUPESTRIAN ETRURIA

95 San Giovenale
96 Blera
96 Norchia
98 Castel d'Asso
98 Tuscania
100 Acquarossa

102 Funerary Architecture

105 THE VALLEYS OF THE
FIORA AND ALBEGNA

105 Sovana
109 Poggio Buco
109 Castro
110 Saturnia

111 Ghiaccio Forte
111 Magliano
112 Marsiliana d'Albegna
112 Doganella
113 Talamone

116 Roads and Means
of Transport

119 THE MAJOR CENTERS
OF THE TUSCAN COAST

119 Populonia
124 Vetulonia
128 Accesa
129 Roselle

132 Techniques of Goldsmithry

135 THE SIENESE
VALDICHIANA
AND THE VALLEY
OF THE OMBRONE

135 Chiusi
139 Chianciano
142 Sarteano
146 Murlo
147 Asciano

148 The Cult of Water
149 The Museo Archeologico
Nazionale in Chiusi

155 EASTERN ETRURIA

156 Cortona
160 Castiglion Fiorentino
160 Arezzo
165 Pieve a Socana
165 Perugia
168 Todi

170 The *Tabula Cortonensis*
and Land Law

173 VOLTERRA AND THE
SURROUNDING REGION

174 The Origins of Volterra
175 Vada
175 The Territory of Volterra
and Casale Marittimo
178 Volterra from the Archaic
Period to Romanization
181 The Late Settlements
of the Territory

182 Arms and the Army
185 The Museo Etrusco
Guarnacci in Volterra

191 BETWEEN THE ARNO
AND THE APENNINES

191 Prehistory at Sesto
Fiorentino and in the Mugello
192 The Origins of Florence
194 Quinto Fiorentino

196 Artimino and Comeana
198 The Formation of the First
Urban Center at Fiesole
200 Gonfienti
200 The Pressure of the Celts
and Romanization

202 Textiles and Clothing
204 The Museo Archeologico
Nazionale in Florence

209 THE NORTHERN COAST
OF THE TYRRHENIAN
SEA

209 Prehistory
210 Pisa
212 Versilia and the Lucca Region
215 The Settlements of the Period
of Roman Colonization

217 THE ETRUSCANS
OF THE PO VALLEY

217 Bologna
218 Verucchio
219 The Etruscanization of the
Po Valley and Marzabotto
222 Spina, Adria and the Other
Centers

223 Essential Bibliography

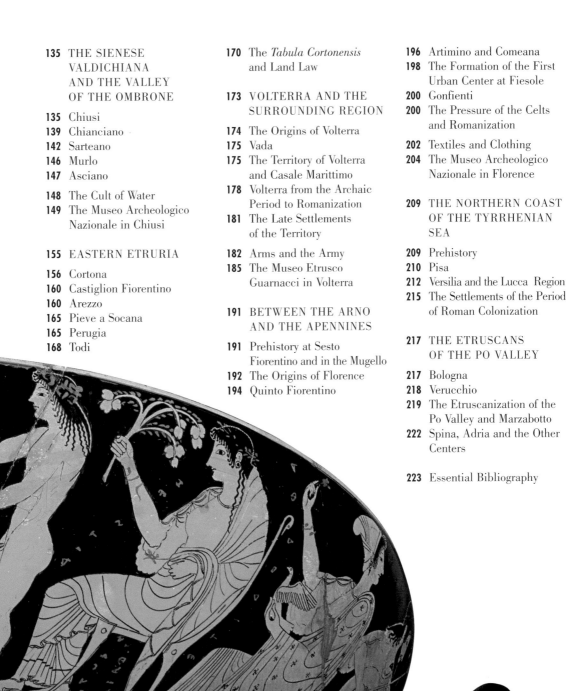

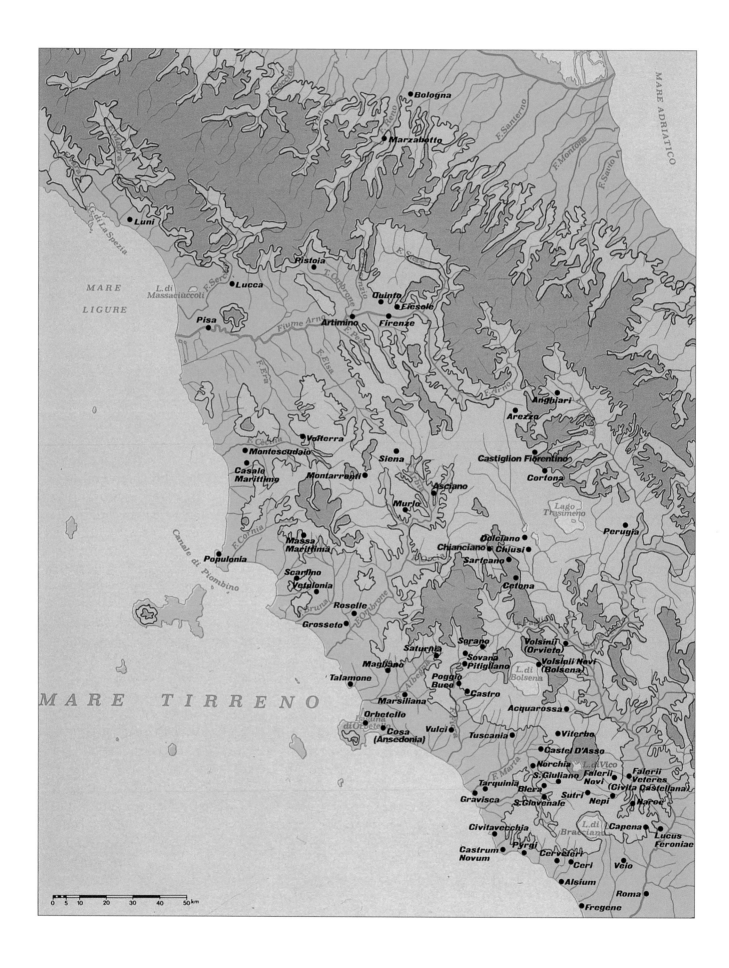

INTRODUCTION

The area traditionally referred to as Etruria in the Latin literary sources was a vast swathe of territory in Central Italy, comprised between the Tiber River to the south, the Arno River to the north and the Apennines to the east. Modern archeological research, while retaining the name of Etruria proper for this region (along with the lands between the Arno and the ridge of the Apennines), has clearly demonstrated that other areas, lying outside this already large expanse, were united with it from very remote times. We should in fact remember that the Etruscan civilization lasted for around a millennium, and that the territory it covered was inevitably fluid, as was the very concept of "Etruria," not to be confused with the modern definition of a territorial state. At the beginning of the Iron Age, the period from which date the vestiges of so-called "Villanovan" culture, an organic part of the Etruscan one, there were no central government, no single body of law and no generally recognized borders. The peoples of antiquity did recognize the existence of areas that could be identified on the basis of common ethnic and cultural aspects (similar biological origins, identity of language and traditions). These were used to distinguish an *ethnos* scattered over a territory, and thus one with ample regional variables that sometimes corresponded to deep sociopolitical divisions.

Thus the Etruscan civilization emerged in the 9th cent. BC in a wilderness characterized by dense patches of scrub and forests on the hillsides, while large areas of cultivable land were located in the valleys. In this area, now occupied by Tuscany and parts of Lazio and Umbria, the environment is dominated by the foothills of the Apennines, the Metallifere Mountains and the massifs of Amiata, Cetona and the Tolfa Mountains. The most characteristic elements of the landscape are the gently rolling hills of Tuscany and the great tufaceous terraces of Lazio. Also typical are the broad river valleys, which link up with the vast plain of the Maremma in the coastal zone, and the more modest ones of the Lazio seaboard, which over the centuries were rendered particularly fertile by a careful optimization of the water regime. The region that was inhabited by the Etruscans comprised bodies of fresh water of volcanic formation (the Lakes of Bolsena, Bracciano and Vico) or tectonic origin, like the huge Lake Trasimeno.

From the outset the Etruscan culture appears to have been quite distinct from the contemporary ones of Greece, by which it was deeply influenced, and Rome, which on the contrary absorbed traditions and customs from the Etruscans: in fact the language is totally different, even though its alphabet is derived from Greek, just as the marked religiosity, the fascination with the world of the dead and the conservative tendency in an aristocratic sense are all peculiar to the culture. Greek and Roman writers called attention to the problem of the origin of the Etruscans, launching a prolific debate that has continued for over two thousand years. According to the historian Herodotus (5th cent. BC), they had arrived from Lydia, in the Eastern Mediterranean, and had colonized the fertile region facing onto the Tyrrhenian Sea. The migration had been provoked by a severe famine in their country of origin and ordered by Tyrsenos, the king's son. This legendary provenance served to ennoble the refined civilization

Impasto hut urn from
the Cavalupo Necropolis,
Vulci, 9th cent. BC.
Museo Nazionale Etrusco
di Villa Giulia, Rome

Cinerary urn
in bronze plate
from Falerii Veteres,
mid-7th cent. BC.
Museo Nazionale Etrusco
di Villa Giulia, Rome

by deriving it from the Greek world. In the late 1st cent. BC, on the other hand, Dionysius of Halicarnassus claimed that the Etruscans were an ancient indigenous population, unlike the Romans who stemmed from a mixture of different peoples, although all of Greek origin, stressing the absolute uniqueness of their customs and language with respect to other populations of Italy. For a long time a series of arguments was put forward to support or confute one of these two theories. Today it is thought that the civilization was an exceptional blend of cultural influences from the outside (the Mediterranean and Central Europe) with a local ethnic group, invigorated by the influx – partly through immigration – of several small minorities. Given the complexity of this process of formation by assimilation, much research now focuses on investigating the mechanisms by which the Etruscan culture was created.

So in the 11th cent. BC the first groups of huts made their appearance in the large expanse of territory between the valleys of the Tiber and the Arno, occupying naturally fortified plateaus, bounded and defended by steep walls of rock. It is only recently that the modest traces of these settlements which have survived, consisting of hearths and holes for the posts used to support the structures of wood, straw and clay, have begun to be investigated. The outward appearance of these humble dwellings is documented by various examples of hut urns: found only inside pit tombs located in certain areas, these were made of bronze or *impasto*, an

Impasto ossuary
from Volterra, 9th-8th
cent. BC. Museo Etrusco
Guarnacci, Volterra

Impasto urn with helmet-
shaped lid from the
Montarano Necropolis,
Falerii Veteres,
mid-8th cent. BC.
Museo Nazionale Etrusco
di Villa Giulia, Rome

unrefined clay containing sand, small pieces of stone, straw and other organic matter. The cremation burials of this period, made in holes dug in the ground, contain biconical ossuaries covered with bowls and modest grave goods. Yet there was already a tendency to characterize the sex of the deceased: spindle whorls connected with the activity of spinning were placed in women's graves and rare weapons in those of men. Even more sporadic are the hut urns and ossuaries covered with bronze or clay helmets (in some cases accompanied by spears and swords), respectively representing the activities of a head of family with sacred functions and those of a warrior. The presence of artifacts made in nuraghic Sardinia in the tombs shows that there must have been at least some degree of trade with other cultures.

In the late 8th cent. BC the burials begin to show clear signs of a social structure that was taking on a clan-based character, i.e. made up of large groups of families united by their descent from a common ancestor, within which chattels and lands were inherited, thanks to the diffusion of private as opposed to collective property. This organization of society, together with the use of iron tools, explains the flourishing of agriculture, practiced on land located in the immediate vicinity of the settlements, with particular emphasis on the cultivation of cereals and pulses.

The communities of the Late Iron Age lived in very large agglomerates that were transformed over the following decades into the large coastal cities of Caere, Tarquinii, Veii, Vulci and Vetulonia, which underwent a spectacular flowering over the course of the 7th century. In Northern Etruria, on the other hand, the phenomenon of aggregation appears to have been much slower and less striking. In fact the location of the coastal centers of Southern Etruria on the new routes of trade and communication made them magnets for the surrounding villages and was the cause of the progressive formation of true cities. Consequently these were created through the fusion of groups with different origins, traditions and civil and religious practices, which found common rules of living in the laws laid down by a single king and an assembly of notables (figure with a high social standing). By contrast the population of Northern Etruria, more conservative partly because of its predominant reliance on agriculture, remained scattered over the territory for a longer time, divided up into small principalities based on farming and commerce on a local scale.

Thus the closing decades of the 8th cent. BC brought a progressive change in the makeup of society in Southern Etruria, with the emergence of prosperous upper classes that over the course of the following century would display their wealth by means of lavish tombs covered by monumental mounds. These typified the Etruscan agrarian landscape in the centers on the southern coast as well as in the inland areas as far as Cortona and the valley of the Arno, underlining the power of an "aristocratic" class whose wealth stemmed from the ownership of land, often conquered by acts of war. This was what is known as the "Orientalizing" period on the grounds of the strong cultural and artistic influences coming from the Eastern Mediterranean, documented by the import of valuable pottery and metal ware, and by the imitation of their forms, ornamentation and figurative repertoire in the Italic area. In Etruria this period was to last from the late 8th century right up until the end of the 7th.

The large burial mounds stand in isolation or in groups, forming imposing necropolises like that of the Banditaccia at Cerveteri, with bases carved out of the tufa and decorated with moldings, against which were set altars for sacrifices in honor of the gods of the underworld. Large tumuli also stood on the shores of the small bay of Baratti, at the foot of the hill of Populonia, while on the hillsides of Vetulonia the funeral monuments were delimited by a circle of stones driven into the ground: inside them, the graves of high-ranking personages were located in large pits.

pp. 8-9: The Banditaccia necropolis with burial mounds, Cerveteri

The tombs of nobles who had been cremated, on the model of the Homeric heroes, contain rich grave goods, including exotic objects, pottery and other lavishly adorned artifacts that reflect the great affluence attained by this aristocratic class. The same elite was the owner of luxurious dwellings, as the extraordinary discoveries made at Murlo and Acquarossa have shown. These were vast, palatial structures with clay tile roofs and richly decorated exteriors intended to demonstrate the power of the aristocratic family, which was already exercised over limited social groups. A memory of the interior of these houses, which mark a clear break with the modest huts of previous centuries, survives in the contemporary chamber tombs, conceived as the abode of the deceased, with mortuary cells linked together by a large vestibule and doors, ceilings, pillars, columns and furnishings in imitation of the houses of the living.

The home life of aristocratic families was conducted in various rooms, some of them used for the working of wool and the production of food. In this connection the literary sources record the raising of livestock, especially pigs, sheep and goats, as an important economic resource of Etruria, although recent archeological research has placed the accent on the fundamental role

Detail of cinerary urn with banqueting scene from Chiusi, last decades of the 6th cent. BC. Museo Archeologico Nazionale, Florence

played by cattle breeding in agriculture. Etruscan racehorses, ridden bareback as can be seen in some contemporary images, were famous too.

Lavish banquets were held in the luxurious houses of the "princes." They are recorded on several terracotta slabs from Acquarossa, and in the words of the philosopher Posidonius of Apamea: "the Etruscans eat twice a day at sumptuous tables, with everything that contributes to a refined life, and are attended by a swarm of servants." The consumption of wine and scented oils, in addition to testifying to the cultivation of vines and olives that was to characterize the landscape of Etruria forever after, reflects the lifestyle of the high-ranking members of society, who tended to assimilate the customs of the Greek and Oriental world. The luxuriant vegetation that covered large parts of Etruria provided plentiful food for wild boar, which were hunted to the sound of the flute and whose meat was greatly appreciated at aristocratic tables. More in general, the opulent meals of this elite included numerous kinds of game that were hunted on the lakes and rivers of the interior, whose abundance of fish is also mentioned in the literary sources. Fishing was extensively practiced at sea, with net, line and spear, as is documented in the Hunting and Fishing Tomb at Tarquinia, while other images on crockery (in particular a plate made at Caere and now in the Museo di Villa Giulia in Rome) depict the use of harpoons to capture large fish, perhaps identifiable as tuna. The guests at an Etruscan banquet were entertained by flute and lyre players and their great appreciation of music is recorded by the iconographic and literary sources, which show that it was performed at religious ceremonies, sporting events and numerous moments of everyday life.

Certainly no less distinctive than the customs, the Etruscan language has stirred fierce debate and controversy, commencing with the alphabet and the practice of writing from right to left. In reality the letters of the alphabet already in use in the 7th cent. BC are of the Western Greek type, the same as is known from several inscriptions at Pithecussae and Cumae, the first Hellenic colonies in the West, and reading it poses no problems at all, although it should be pointed out that in the oldest epigraphs there are no dividing marks between the individual words, which only came into common use in the 6th century. The vast majority of the over ten thousand known inscriptions contain indications of an onomastic and funerary character, while some of the longer texts (the so-called "Zagreb mummy wrapping," a strip of linen cloth from the 3rd-2nd cent. BC on which about 1350 words are written, or the 5th-cent.-BC clay tablet

Detail of terracotta slab with banqueting scene from Acquarossa, 6th cent. BC. Museo Civico, Viterbo

found at Capua with its 390 words) are ritual calendars with indications of sacred formulas and ceremonies to be carried out on particular dates and in honor of specific deities. Other fairly long inscriptions from the 3rd-2nd cent. BC, such as the travertine memorial stone from San Manno, with 128 words, and the bronze tablet called the *Tabula cortonensis*, with 206 words, are of a legal character, concerning a verdict in a dispute over a piece of farmland at Perugia and a transaction also involving land near Cortona respectively. There is also a bilingual text datable to around 500 BC, written in Etruscan and Phoenician on three gold plaques found in the sanctuary of Pyrgi, with a dedication by the local ruler to the goddess *Uni-Astarte*.

A trace of similarity between Etruscan and other languages of the Mediterranean has been detected in some inscriptions discovered on the island of Lemnos: the best-known and longest is on a stele with the figure of a warrior, and consists of 33 words that show remarkable affinities with Etruscan, to the point of suggesting that speakers of the language were present on the Greek island.

The wealth of Etruria also derived from the existence of major mineral deposits on its territory. These attracted Hellenic peoples very early on, fostering processes of economic and cul-

tural development among the emerging local classes. As a consequence several urban centers appeared on the coast toward the end of the 7th cent. BC, and within a short space of time attained a considerable size due to the rapid growth of their population. This was the prelude to what is called the "Archaic" period, corresponding to the years between the end of the 7th and the middle of the 5th cent. BC. It was a time characterized by the definitive formation of cities and, in art, a style of Greek-Oriental inspiration resembling the Ionic in which figures were mostly portrayed in profile, with almond-shaped eyes and the so-called "Etruscan smile." Once it had attained its definitive structure, the organization of the city-state under the leadership of highly active aristocratic groups brought with it a development of agriculture along speculative lines and the growth of commercial activities connected with trade in the products of the fertile territory: cereals, wine and oil, with the latter particularly favored by the hilly terrain.

It was in this period too that the southern Etruscan cities located on broad plateaus in view of the sea created specialized port facilities on the coast, giving a further boost to the development of mercantile activities. It was from here, in fact, that vessels set sail for new trade routes, with the result that the sea onto which the region faced became known as the Tyrrhenian, after *Tyrrhenoi*, the Greek name for the Etruscans.

Etruscan mariners, according to the sources, were much feared and renowned for legendary exploits such as the theft of the statue of Hera from the island of Samos. The Greeks considered them pirates for the bold deeds they carried out in the Mediterranean, and the eighth Homeric Hymn dedicated to Dionysus told how Etruscans had succeeded in capturing the ship on which the god of wine was traveling incognito. Dionysus had then freed himself by turning the Tyrrhenian sailors into dolphins. In reality, such myths reflected the great commercial rivalry between the Greek and Etruscan peoples over the control of sea routes and the wine trade.

Hand in hand with the increase in trade went an expansion in manufacturing activities in the vicinity of such major South Etruscan centers as Caere. Workshops appeared producing large quantities of pottery, including the characteristic black *bucchero* ware with stamped geometric decorations or the figures of real and fantastic creatures. Images drawn from mythology were rare, but with the passing of the decades the decoration of the pots became more lavish, covering the entire surface. Some of these workshops were run by skilled potters from Greece, such as Demaratus of Corinth who came to Tarquinii around the middle of the 7th cent. BC, bringing other craftsmen with him. Demaratus played an important role not just in the history of the Etruscan city, where he is said to have introduced the figurative arts and writing, but also in that of Rome, as he was the father of its future king Lucius Tarquinius Priscus. And it was this Tarquin who brought customs derived from Etruscan culture to the city on the Tiber, taking from Etruria (according to the literary tradition) such insignia of supreme power as the fasces with the axes of the lictors, the curule chair, the war trumpet and the toga bordered with purple.

Other centers like Vetulonia produced fine gold artifacts of exquisite Orientalizing taste, while the bronze work of Vulci was highly appreciated by the aristocracy and earned praise even in Greece. The reputation of the metal objects produced in Etruria is underlined by the story that one of the Thirty Tyrants in 5th-century Athens longed to possess an entire service made in the Etruscan bronze workshops. They are also mentioned by the Athenian playwright Pherecrates, who has one of his characters declare: these candlesticks "are Etruscan, for the Etruscans, lovers of the fine arts, do really excellent work." In the area of Campiglia, in the "industrial" quarter of Baratti at the foot of Populonia and above all on the island of Elba fires were lit for the roasting and smelting of iron ore, producing tall plumes of smoke that prompted the Greeks to call the island Aethalia ("Smoky Place").

The economic growth of the various urban centers, to which we have already referred, also resulted in a redistribution of wealth among several family groups. Unequivocal evidence for this is provided by funerary architecture, with the increase in the number of monumental tombs, and the import of figured Greek pottery on a large scale. The latter proves to have been an important means of familiarization with customs from outside Etruria and with myths, narrated in detail, that led to the introduction of Hellenic cultural models as well as an interest in Greek literature. It is in this perspective we should see the arrival of the monumental *François Vase* (Museo Archeologico, Florence), a masterpiece of Attic ceramics by the painter Cleitias and the potter Ergotimos that is adorned with a series of images of extraordinary interest and characterized by an otherwise unknown wealth of detail.

During this cultural phase (6th cent. BC), the political organization of Etruria was based on an alliance of twelve independent city states (perhaps on the model of the Ionian League), sometimes in conflict with one another, that exercised their control over territories whose boundaries cannot be established with certainty. Their representatives used to meet at annual ceremonies where a number of deities were venerated through solemn sacrifices and sporting contests. Held at the federal sanctuary of Voltumna near Volsinii, these set the seal on the ethnic and religious league of the "Twelve Peoples of Etruria." These can in all likelihood be identified as the cities of Veii (Veio), Caere (Cerveteri), Tarquinii (Tarquinia), Vulci, Rusellae (Roselle), Vetulonia, Volsinii (Orvieto), Clusium (Chiusi), Perusia (Perugia), Cortona, Arretium (Arezzo) and Volterra. Populonia was only added to the list after the destruction of Veii by the Romans (396 BC), although the archeological evidence seems to indicate a great prosperity that cannot easily be reconciled with the absence of this city from the ceremonies at the Volsinian sanctuary before the 4th century. The council held at Volsinii also elected a priest to preside over the festivities in

Detail of bucchero *aryballos* with inscription from Vulci, 7th cent. BC. Museo Nazionale Etrusco di Villa Giulia, Rome

honor of the gods, and it was at that assembly, according to Livy, that a nail was driven into the wall of the shrine dedicated to Nortia, to keep count of the years and the slow passing of time. That the small territorial states, whose size and density of population must have changed over the course of the centuries, enjoyed a high degree of autonomy is apparent from various accounts, including those relating to the capitulation of Veii. In fact Livy tells us that, at the Fanum Voltumnae, the city twice asked for help from the other Etruscan peoples in its war with Rome but was turned down each time, with the result that, left to its own devices, it was defeated and destroyed by the nascent Roman power.

The aforementioned Etruscan presence on the seas, permitting control of the main trade routes, was temporarily eclipsed by the foundation, between the beginning and middle of the 6th century, of Phocaean colonies at Massalia (Marseilles) on the French coast and Alalia (Aleria) on the Tyrrhenian shore of Corsica. This was perceived as a threat to the commercial expansion of coastal Etruria, and around 540 BC a large Etruscan fleet, in alliance with Carthage, clashed with the Phocaeans, inflicting a crushing victory on them off the coast of Corsica. This put a permanent check on commercial Greek settlements in this part of the Mediterranean, as well as favoring the Etruscan penetration of the southern Tyrrhenian Sea. According to the sources the main burden of the war was borne by Caere, at that time the principal maritime power of Etruria, which expressed its gratitude to the gods with the dedication of a *thesauros* of its own at the sanctuary of Delphi.

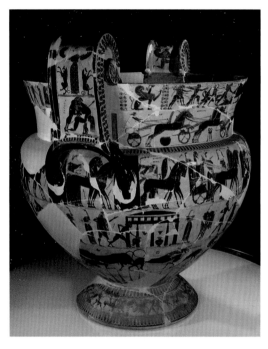

François Vase from Fonte Rotella, Chiusi, 560 BC. Museo Archeologico, Florence; opposite, detail

The demographic picture presented by Southern Etruria in this period shows a depopulation of the countryside, with the abandonment of numerous minor settlements, while the major coastal centers underwent a massive increase in population connected with the flourishing of trade. Some cities were ringed with high walls and in many centers there are signs of a spurt of construction, with rich decorations embellishing buildings of a religious and public nature. Sacred complexes were erected on tall podia and elegantly adorned with polychrome terracottas, and sometimes with statues of deities set on the pediment or on top of the roof. The profile was enlivened with plant motifs and rows of heads of women and men, or of fantastic beings, located at the ends of the pantiles of the roof (antefixes).

There were particularly active workshops devoted to the production of architectural terracottas at Caere and Veii, as the finding of numerous slabs, acroteria and large clay statues testify. The skill of the craftsmen of Caere also found expression in the creation of such extraordinary works as sarcophagi with figures of the married couple reclining on the lid.

As usual, the necropolises offer clues to the urban society of the closing decades of the 6th century, reflecting the prosperity that Etruria enjoyed. Cultural exchanges with the Greek and Oriental world appear to have been intense and the tombs at Tarquinii started to be decorated with extraordinary cycles of paintings influenced by the Ionic style. In these paintings the banquet in the open air or with the guests reclining on luxurious beds (held on the occasion of the funeral of the founder of the tomb) is a lavish display of luxury, intended to reflect the wealth of the deceased, who is depicted among the diners as if still alive, serenely honored by his family, attended by servants and entertained by lively dancers and dignified musicians.

The situation in Northern Etruria, where cities like Arretium, Faesulae (Fiesole) and

Volterra were located a great distance apart, was different. The countryside does not seem to have experienced extreme forms of desertion. On the contrary, some of the secondary centers flourished, keeping essentially in step with the larger towns and cities. The affluence of the Northern Etruscan landowning aristocracy was based on skilful exploitation of agricultural resources and it showed its enterprise by colonizing Northern Italy, with vast movements of migration into the Emilian and Lombard regions in search of new markets. In fact it was due to the initiative of the aristocratic class of some of the inland city states of Central and Northern Etruria, especially Clusium, that the territories of the Po Valley were colonized, a fact supported by the literary tradition, which attributes the foundation of Felsina (Bologna) to a certain Aucnus from Perusia.

It is to this moment that the Latin historian Titus Livius must have been referring when he said that the power of the Etruscans was widespread on land and sea, extending beyond the limits of the region as far as the Po Valley and the fertile lands of Campania, where the territory was organized into a league of twelve cities like Etruria proper.

The craftsmanship of Central and Northern Etruria appears to have been strongly influenced by developments in Southern Etruria and the upper classes liked to show off their bronze vessels and Attic vases.

Etruscan decorative traditions were adopted in Rome too, and it was the last of the Tarquins, Lucius Tarquinius Superbus, who erected the great sanctuary of Capitoline Jupiter, sumptuously adorned by Vulca and other craftsmen from Veii. The end of the Etruscan dynasty came in 509 BC, when Tarquin the Proud was expelled and took refuge with Aristodemus, tyrant of Cumae, while the republic was established in Rome. This was the background to the venture of Porsenna, described by the literary sources as ruler of Clusium and Volsinii, who in an attempt to reinstall Tarquin the Proud in Rome, occupied the city for a brief span of time, something that is testified by the ban on the use of iron for anything but the manufacture of agricultural implements imposed on the Romans.

At the start of the 5th century Etruscan maritime power appears to have still been in the ascendant, and as a consequence trade in expansion, but shortly afterward the situation was to change radically, with serious repercussions for the fate of

Apollo of Veii from the sanctuary of Portonaccio, late 6th cent. BC. Museo Nazionale Etrusco di Villa Giulia, Rome

Etruria. In 474 BC, in fact, a heavy naval defeat was inflicted on the southern coastal cities off Cumae by Hieron of Syracuse, who intervened in support of the Cumaeans with a fleet of triremes that wiped out the Etruscan ships. A clear record of the victory, celebrated by Pindar in the *Pythian Odes*, survives in the offering of bronze helmets found in the sanctuary of Zeus at Olympia with an inscription dedicating it to the Syracusan triumph. This marked the beginning of a progressive decline in the Etruscan presence in the Tyrrhenian, which was to continue over the course of the century as further blows were dealt by the forces of Syracuse. These resulted in a great deterioration of the economy of the cities on the coast, which were no longer capable of sustaining their trade, and a consequent weakening of their political power that led to the loss of the cities in Campania.

Diodorus Siculus recounts that in 453 BC Syracuse came into conflict with the cities of Etruria again, and two naval expeditions were sent to the island of Elba to oppose what the Greeks defined as Etruscan piracy. The first attack under the command of the navarch Phaillos was limited to a raid on the island, as the Etruscans succeeded in bribing him, while the second with sixty triremes led by Apelles was devastating and accompanied by ruthless pillaging. Following these tragic events the island in the Tuscan archipelago and various coastal settlements were equipped with fortresses to control the sea lanes, but the decline of Etruscan maritime power had now become inexorable. A final and decisive blow was inflicted at the time of the failed siege of Syracuse (415-413 BC), which saw the participation of an Etruscan military contingent alongside the forces of Athens. The heavy defeats suffered at the hands of the Syracusans, together with complicated internal phenomena of a social nature, resulted in a collapse of imports and economic crisis in the coastal cities. This is evident in both public building and the production of handicrafts, which came to an abrupt halt. However, the inland centers of Etruria maintained a high level of prosperity, testified by the sacred architecture that was given new impetus at Volsinii and Clusium.

The second half of the century was also marked by hostilities between Rome and Veii, which had begun several decades earlier and then flared up again over the possession of Fidenae. In fact the town, located strategically at a ford on the Tiber River, was considered to be of fundamental importance to Roman expansion into the Sabine and Umbrian regions. Its siege and destruction by the Romans in 426 BC was the spark for the rekindling of the war with Veii, studded with frequent military clashes that were to continue for many years, with alternate fortunes. Abandoned to its fate by the marked individualism of the other Etruscan cities, despite repeated calls for assistance, Veii was definitively overcome in 396 BC after a long siege. With the annexation of its territory, Rome had at last succeeded in crossing over to the right bank of the Tiber, which no longer served as its boundary. The way was now clear for the conquest of the whole of Etruria.

But danger signals were also coming from across the Alps. In fact at the beginning of the 4th cent. BC Gaulish tribes occupied the fertile zones of the Po Valley and had no difficulty in seizing the centers founded by the Etruscans, with the exception of Mantua, putting an end to their domination of Northern Italy. Shortly afterward a group of Senones reached Etruria, perhaps attracted by the rich products of the countryside. In his monumental history of Rome, Livy claims that the Celtic tribe of the Senones had come to Clusium on the instigation of Arruns, an ordinary citizen who had not been able to bear the seduction of his wife by a local prince. The story, despite its overtones of romance, seems to hint at conflict between the city's elites and underlines the extent of the trade that had been established between the fertile Val di Chiana and Northern Italy. In this situation the intervention of Roman ambassadors, sought by the rulers of Clusium, prompted the attack of the Senones on Rome, which was burned and destroyed, to such an extent that its inhabitants may have moved to nearby Veii. Thanks to the plebeian Lucius Albinius the flamen priests (administrators of the worship of the gods), the Vestal virgins and the sacred vessels of the Roman religion were saved and transferred to Caere, a city "allied" with Rome but with no voting rights.

At the end of the first two decades of the 4th century the picture was essentially that of a weakened region which had lost control of its territories in Campania and to the north of the Apennines. Its mercantile marine activity was much reduced and some of the coastal cities had fallen back on an agricultural economy, with a consequent reoccupation of the countryside. One of the most lively reactions to this situation came from Tarquinii, whose territory was in the front line of the Roman offensive. The city was ruled by Aule Spurinna, a figure of high social rank and considerable political stature, whose actions were focused on both Southern Etruria, with the deposition of King Orgolnius of Caere, and the northern territories, with the dispatch of the army to put down a slave revolt at Arretium. The offensive he led against the Romans between 358 and 351 BC produced no positive result, however, concluding in a forty-year truce following a very bloody episode, the killing of three hundred Roman prisoners in the forum of Tarquinii.

The rich heritage of wall paintings that began to appear in the tombs of Tarquinii from the 4th century onward testifies to a radical change in figurative programs, closely linked with political developments. The banquet was transferred from the traditional setting of the world of the living to that of the next world, i.e. to the dark abode of Hades, inhabited by the dead, and the guests now included gods of the underworld, demons and ancestors.

Detail of bronze lebes
(urn) from Capua,
early 5th cent. BC.
British Museum, London

Over the course of the century Etruscan history was marked by the end of the forty years of peace with the Romans (311-310 BC). As had already happened in the previous war, the Etruscans concentrated their attacks on Sutri, a border stronghold now within the orbit of Rome and a staging post on the route between the Lakes of Vico and Bracciano. Several cities of Northern Etruria, but not Arretium, sent military contingents. The most important contribution was made by Perusia and Volsinii, which at that moment played a dominant role in the Etruscan league and had close ties with the other cities of the region, as the inscriptions in Tomb Golini I at Orvieto demonstrate.

An echo of the fierce battles between Etruscans and Romans, linked to those of the heroes of Greek mythology, can be seen in the extraordinary pictorial decoration of the François Tomb at Vulci, where Vel Saties, the probable founder of the tomb, reveals the final outcome of the conflict through the divinatory practice of the observation of birds in flight.

The century closed with a popular insurrection at Arretium in which the lower classes rose against the families of the local oligarchy, and which was only suppressed through the intervention of Roman troops led by Marcus Valerius Maximus, something that hints at a pro-Roman attitude on the part of some of the local aristocracy. The overwhelming power of Roman military organization at the beginning of the 3rd century could no longer be contained. The crushing defeat at Sentinum (295 BC) toward the end of the Samnite Wars marked the beginning of the end for many Etruscan cities.

The following year Rome invaded the territory of Volsinii, laying waste to it and leaving 2800 dead, and then turned its attention to Rusellae, sacking the city, killing 2000 men and taking the same number prisoner. Roman forces had now penetrated deep into Etruscan territory, and the ore deposits of the Metallifere Mountains were the next to be conquered. Between 282 and 273 BC many towns and cities were subdued and the *fasti triumphales* (lists of the triumphs of Roman generals) of 280 record the victory of Tiberius Coruncanius over Volsinii and Vulci, which probably lost their independence. In the following years Populonia and Volterra were also conquered by the Romans, while much of the territory of Caere was confiscated.

Various colonies would be founded in the coastal area: Alsium, Fregenae, Pyrgi, and Castrum Novum (Santa Marinella) in the territory of Caere, Gravisca in that of Tarquinii and Cosa in that of Vulci, sometimes occupying sites that had been used as landing places and in other cases shifting the centers of power that exercised control over the territory. No better was the fate of the inland cities of Etruria, forced to make peace under extremely harsh terms.

A famous passage from Livy's history presents a picture of the situation of Etruria at the turn of the century, describing Scipio's promise of aid on the part of the cities of Etruria, now allied with Rome, for a new military campaign against Hannibal. The city of Caere offered wheat and other provisions for the fleet, Tarquinii just canvas for the ships, Pupluna iron, Volterra grain and wax for the vessels, Perusia, Clusium and Rusellae cereals and timber for shipbuilding. Arretium on the other hand, which controlled the mining region of the Rognosi Mountains and enjoyed a certain prosperity, supplied the Romans with 3000 shields, 3000 helmets and 50 000 spears, as well as hoes, sickles and everything needed to fit out 40 ships.

It is clear that Roman control was now total, although its effects were expressed in different ways. The southern region, with its formerly wealthy coastal cities and minor settlements destroyed by the Roman troops, saw the confiscation of large portions of the territories of Vulci, Caere and Tarquinii. By contrast the inland parts of Southern Etruria, and in particular the area of the rupestrian necropolises, characterized by the monumental façades of tombs carved out of the rock, underwent a fairly significant increase in population between the final decades

Opposite, head of Aita (Hades) in the Orcus II Tomb, first half of the 4th cent. BC., Tarquinia

of the 4th cent. BC and the 3rd, ascribable to a more intensive exploitation of agriculture. Several centers appear to have been inhabited by a wealthy class of landowning aristocracy, and the funerary epigraphs of some of its members boast of the high public posts they held at Tarquinii. Another important factor was the opening of the Via Clodia by the Romans, linking Rome with Saturnia and encouraging the development of small settlements and construction of scattered rural buildings.

The presence of a middle to upper class is also recognizable in the cemeteries of this period at Tarquinii, characterized by carefully planned tombs with several depositions as at Caere. For inhumations sarcophagi were produced with a figure of the deceased reclining at a banquet on the lid, in "heroic" seminudity in the oldest examples, or dressed in a cloak and tunic in those of the 2nd cent. BC. The subsequent economic resources of aristocratic families is reflected by the presence in the tombs of painted decorations, usually depicting subjects related to the underworld. The afterlife appears to be populated by monstrous creatures, and there are frequent scenes of a procession to the other world for the tombs of local magistrates of the city aristocracy, extolling the role played by the deceased in society.

The anxieties to which that society was evidently prone were further increased by the strong tensions that emerged in it over the course of the 2nd century. An echo of this can still be seen in the clay figures of the decoration of the temple at Telamon (Talamone), representing the fratricidal struggle between Eteocles and Polyneices. The Roman designs on Etruscan territory also led to the founding of the colony of Saturnia in 183 BC and that of Heba (Magliano) at an unknown date. The aim behind the foundation of such colonies was to integrate the former territory of Vulci into that of Rome in a definitive manner.

"Sarcophagus of the Magistrate" from Tarquinii, late 3rd - early 2nd cent. BC. Museo Archeologico Nazionale, Tarquinia

We are now at the height of the Hellenistic era, a period characterized by the spread of a distinctive combination of Greek and Oriental culture through the Mediterranean region, following the creation of Alexander the Great's empire. The phase is conventionally held to correspond to the years between Alexander's death (323 BC) and 31 BC, the date of the battle of Actium and the conquest of Egypt by Rome. In this period inland Northern Etruria, the area comprised between Perusia, Clusium and Volterra, presents a very positive economic picture: an increase in the activities of artisans and agricultural production, with a consequent rise in population and expansion of the "middle" class, with a high level of literacy, living on small farms of just a few hectares. In the first few decades of the 2nd cent. BC, however, these vast swathes of territory were also affected by social tensions deriving from attempts to transform the relations between classes and the demand for integration of the lower strata of society, denied political rights. This process seems to have reached a conclusion in the second half of the century, with different results in the various areas, so that the countryside around Perusia seems to have been far more closely bound to the city than was that of Clusium or Volterra. In any case the economic model that tended to stem from such conflicts in this northern area was very different from the coastal one. In fact the evidence from the northern cities indicated a different attitude on the part of the Romans, who in these areas did not carry out the confiscation of land that was common in Southern Etruria, where huge estates cultivated by slaves were created, anticipating the system that would be used under the Roman empire.

The tranquil situation that held sway in the Northern Etruscan cities for much of the 2nd century seems to have continued into the beginning of the next, with scanty participation of the Etruscan aristocracy in the revolt that shook the Italian peninsula and led to the granting of Roman citizenship in 89 BC, ratified by the *Lex Julia* and *Lex Calpurnia de civitate*. The following years would be marked by dramatic events of a military and political character. The landing of Marius at the port of Telamon (87 BC) and his enrolment of the rural population, some of them perhaps of Etruscan origin, was to lead to fierce clashes in the subsequent civil war between Marius's and Sulla's forces. Siding with Marius, much of Etruria would suffer destruction and violence as Sulla wreaked his revenge. Even the rural landscape, especially in Northern Etruria, would undergo permanent changes as a result of these events, with the total disappearance of small estates and their replacement by large Roman villas worked by slaves.

From that time on the Latin language took the place of the Etruscan one and in the second half of the 1st century the last great battle took place under the walls of a city in Northern Etruria, Perusia.

The Etruscan ritual books, which have unfortunately not survived but of which an echo has been preserved in other sources, had foretold that the history of the people would last for ten ages of irregular length, called "centuries," and that the passage from one century to another would be marked by the appearance of divine prodigies. In the view of the haruspices, the Augustan era meant that the end was nigh, inasmuch as the last century for the Etruscan *nomen* had begun.

Toward the end of the 1st cent. BC, Augustus's reorganization of the administration had assigned the former territory of Etruria to the Regio VII, bringing a thousand years of Etruscan history to an end. Many of the civilization's customs and usages would be assimilated by the Romans, who had taken the models for their insignia of power or arts of divination from the Etruscans ever since the regal period. In the Augustan age the grandeur of Etruria was to inspire a eulogistic and nostalgic literary genre, fostered by such figures as Maecenas and Virgil, themselves of avowed Etruscan origin. (G.P.)

THE MAJOR CENTERS OF LAZIO

Between the mouth of the Tiber and the promontory of the Argentario, laid out on broad plateaus in view of the sea, stood the principal cities of coastal Etruria; lively commercial centers able to control vast expanses of territory in the hinterland.

The wealth of the southernmost of them, Caere, was linked to flourishing maritime trade, and its name to the production of *bucchero* ware. The fame of Tarquinia, or Tarquinii as the Romans called it, a city of "mythical" foundation, is based on its celebrated painted tombs. Further to the north, Vulci was a center of the production of refined pottery that attests to fertile contacts with the Greek world.

Caere (Cerveteri)

Founded according to tradition by Pelasgian peoples, Caere (Caisria in Etruscan) stood on a vast platform of tufa not far from the sea, only partly occupied by the modern town of Cerveteri. The oldest phase, dating from the Villanovan era, is characterized by modest well tombs, while its great economic, cultural and artistic flowering took place in the Orientalizing period (7th cent. BC), at a time when the city, covering an area of over 150 hectares, became one of the most important in Etruria. Going by the sources and archeological evidence, this exceptional growth seems to have been largely the result of maritime commercial activity, conducted chiefly through the ports of Alsium and Pyrgi. The city played a primary role in trade on the Tyrrhenian Sea, and to defend its interests fought alongside the Carthaginians against the Greeks of Phocaea in a bloody battle off the Corsican coast (540 BC). At the same time, however, it established active links with the Greek world, something which is reflected in the erection of a small shrine (*thesauros*) at the sanctuary of Apollo in Delphi, as well as in the presence of a group of merchants and craftsmen of Hellenic origin in the city.

Caere, unlike other cities in Etruria, also had close contacts with Rome, and at the time of the invasion by the Gauls in 390 BC was chosen by the Romans as a refuge for the Vestal Virgins and Penates. By virtue of this alliance and the assistance it provided, it was granted *civitas sine suffragio*, or "citizenship without voting rights," but in the second half of the 4th century, following the wars between Tarquinii and Rome, relations between the two cities grew increasingly hostile. In 273 it was forced to cede much of its territory in the coastal belt to Rome. It was here that the colonies of Fregenae, Castrum Novum and Pyrgi would be constructed.

The memory of such an important past is preserved today by the necropolises laid out around the city: the vast cemetery of the Banditaccia to the north, the tombs of Monte Abatone to the south and those of the Sorbo to the

Bucchero vase in the form of a warrior's head from the Banditaccia Necropolis, Cerveteri, 7th cent. BC.
Museo Nazionale Etrusco di Villa Giulia, Rome

Opposite and below, sections of the Banditaccia Necropolis at Cerveteri

pp. 26-7: sepulchral street near Large Tumulus II, Banditaccia Necropolis

Interior of the tomb of the Shields and Chairs, mid-7th cent. BC

west, where people were being buried as early as the 9th-8th cent. BC.

The plan of the necropolis of the Banditaccia is of great interest, giving it the characteristics of a true city of the dead, with a paved street onto which face monumental burial mounds, sometimes with altars that were used for ceremonies in honor of the deceased, and lined with more modest tombs in the shape of a "cube" or with a continuous front.

A distinctive feature of the tombs of the Banditaccia is that they provide important clues to the interior of the houses of the living,

offering us a glimpse of the lost domestic architecture of the Etruscans. The oldest tombs imitate the interior of huts, while the larger and more sumptuous ones are based on the dwellings of wealthy aristocrats, with plans that show precise parallels with the structures excavated at Acquarossa.

The graves of women might be marked by stones in the shape of a house and those of men by small columns, sometimes bearing the name of the deceased.

The Tomb of the Hut, with two adjoining rooms and a pitched covering and slender cen-

tral beam that are a realistic reproduction of a thatched roof, is inspired by a hut from the first half of the 7th cent. BC. It is located inside the oldest mound in the necropolis, the large Tumulus II, which also contains the Tomb of the Greek Vases. Like the latter, the Tomb of the Shields and Chairs in the tumulus of the same name offers a precious testimony to the internal structure of houses. It has a large vestibule entered through a *dromos* and is adorned with large carved shields, located above a number of funeral beds and two chairs with high curved backs and footrests set against the rear wall. From this three doors lead to the same number of chambers with pitched roofs and funeral beds along the walls. The Tomb of the Capitals is characterized instead by a room adorned with octagonal columns topped by capitals that support a coffered ceiling. Another tomb of considerable interest is that of the Five Chairs, made up of two small chambers located at the sides of the access corridor. The wall of one of the chambers is lined with five chairs with footrests. Once these must have held terracotta figurines that are now in Rome and London.

The later Tomb of the Alcove, belonging to the Tarnas family and one of the most significant examples of the architecture of Caere in the 4th cent. BC, has a different structure. It consists of a single room with large fluted pillars and has a large bed with footrests on a podium with three steps at the back, perhaps intended for two depositions, those of the founders of the tomb. Again related to the Etruscan architecture of the 4th century is the Tomb of the Reliefs, entered by means of a flight of steps that was decorated with two sculpted lions. The huge mortuary chamber, owned by the Matuna family, has a ceiling with two pitches and a central beam supported by pillars. All around are set large burial niches with cushions, while the walls and the pillars are richly decorated with stucco representations of a large variety of objects that help us to reconstruct the settings of everyday life and the furniture and utensils used in the home.

Some of the graves contain the remains of wall paintings, like the Tumulus of the Animal Paintings which covers four groups of chambers and takes its name from the tomb deco-

Above, nenfro statue of the demon Charun, from Ripe di Sant'Angelo at Cerveteri. Museo Nazionale Cerite, Cerveteri

Interior of the tomb of the Capitals, late 7th cent. BC.; right, tomb of the Five chairs, Banditaccia Necropolis, mid-7th cent. BC

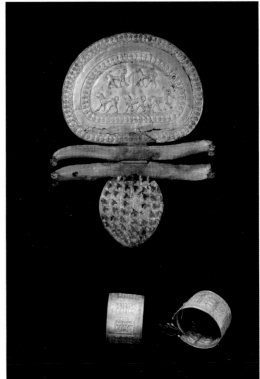

Corridor of the Regolini-Galassi Tomb, Sorbo Necropolis, 7th cent. BC

Large fibula, gold bracelets and bronze cauldron with heads of wild beasts from the Regolini-Galassi Tomb, second quarter of the 7th cent. BC. Museo Gregoriano Etrusco, Vatican

Opposite, interior of the tumulus of the Painted Animals, Banditaccia Necropolis

rated with paintings, including the figure of a lion in the Orientalizing style.

The necropolis of Monte Abatone, very large but less well known than the Banditaccia, houses many tumuli, including the Campana Tomb (7th cent. BC) with a carved ceiling and mock columns on the walls. The later Torlonia Tomb with a façade of the rupestrian type and a huge funerary chamber with large niches at the sides is of great interest. At the back, at the top of two steps, a broad funeral bed must have held the oldest interment.

The best-known tomb in the necropolis of the Sorbo is the one called Regolini-Galassi

(after the names of its discoverers). It consists of a fairly long passageway onto which open two cells covered by a corbel vault that house three depositions. The contents of the grave, now in the Museo Gregoriano Etrusco, are among the richest of the 7th century, and comprise refined objects imported from the East and products of local workshops.

Other significant tombs have been brought to light at the Ripe di Sant'Angelo, from which come two statues representing *Charun*, the Etruscan death demon. Carved from a type of tufa called nenfro, they are on display in the local museum.

Pyrgi

Opposite, detail of clay group with mythological scene from the Theban cycle, from the area of temple A at Pyrgi, mid-5th cent. BC. Museo Nazionale Etrusco di Villa Giulia, Rome

View of the coast at Santa Severa (Pyrgi)

Gold plaques with inscriptions in Etruscan and Phoenician, from sacred area C of Pyrgi, late 6th cent. BC. Museo Nazionale Etrusco di Villa Giulia, Rome

The most important of the ports on the Tyrrhenian coast constructed by Caere was Pyrgi, near Santa Severa, linked to the city by a road lined with large burial mounds. The Etruscan settlement lies underneath the ruins of the colony founded by the Romans, while the remains of the wharves have been identified in front of the Castello degli Orsini. Pyrgi is mentioned by the ancient sources in connection with the sacking of the sanctuary that stood there by Dionysius I of Syracuse in 384 BC, which yielded the considerable sum of a thousand talents. According to Strabo the guardian deity of the temple was Eileithyia, while for the Pseudo-Aristotle, she was Leucothea, protectress of navigation. The sacred area has been discovered a short distance from the sea and excavations have revealed the imposing foundation walls of two places of worship set side by side, built of large squared blocks. Temple B, dated to the end of the 6th cent. BC, has a single cell with a pronaos and colonnaded peristyle. Temple A, datable to the middle of the 5th cent. BC, on a Tuscan plan with a colonnade at the front and three cells at the back, had a rich terracotta decoration with figures from the myth of Thebes, now in the Museo di Villa Giulia in Rome. Also found in the sacred area were the famous gold plaques with inscriptions (two in Etruscan and one in Phoenician) referring to the builder of the sanctuary, King Thefarie Velianas of Caere, and a statue of the goddess Uni, identified with the Phoenician deity Astarte. The bilingual text seems to point to close relations between the Etruscan city and Carthage.

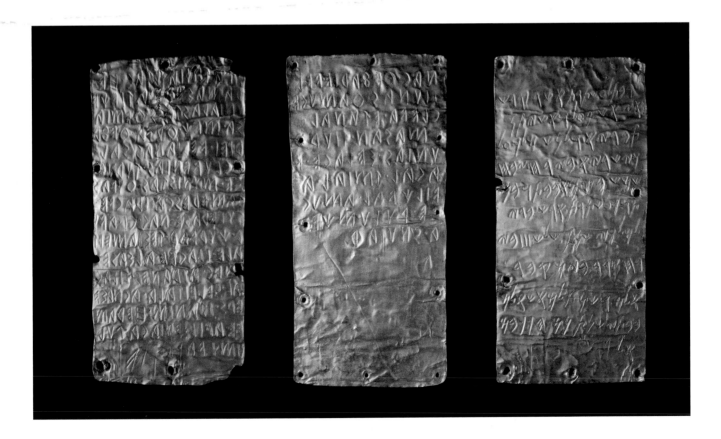

Tarquinii (Tarquinia)

Legend has it that Tarquinii, Tarchuna or Tarchna to the Etruscans, was founded by the mythical Tarchon, the son or brother of Tyrrhenus. The cultural and political preeminence of the city that this story hints at is also conveyed in the sources through the myth of Tages, a figure with the appearance of a child and the wisdom of an old man who sprang from a plowed furrow in the fields near Tarquinii to teach the Etruscans the art of divination by reading the entrails of sacrificed animals.

Substantial vestiges uncovered in the localities of Calvario and Monterozzi attest to the vitality of Tarquinia even in the Villanovan era. Here stood villages of huts that were then abandoned over the course of the 8th cent. BC, when the first nucleus of the Etruscan city was formed on the vast tufaceous plateau of the Civita. Protected on three sides by steep walls, close to the Marta River and just a few kilometers from the coast, the site offered particularly favorable conditions for growth. The contemporary necropolises document the affluence attained by the aristocracy of Tarquinii through the contents of graves belonging to high-ranking personages, such as the pit tomb of the Warrior. Now in Berlin, these included a complete set of armor accompanied by bronzes

Achilles's attack on Troilus, tomb of the Bulls, 530 BC

and pottery of remarkable workmanship. The exceptional grave of a woman known as the chamber Tomb of Bocchoris, with its rich contents now on display at the Museo Archeologico in Tarquinia, dates from later (beginning of the 7th cent. BC).

In close connection with the city's period of economic and cultural splendor, the phenomenon of funerary painting had already began to emerge in the early decades of the 6th century, with simple ornamental decorations executed on the walls of some tombs. It was to become a local pictorial tradition in the second half of the century, when the higher classes drew attention to the social status they had achieved through the refined ornamentation of their own burial chambers. It appears that Greek artists settled in the city had a hand in this decoration.

Among the oldest and best-known examples it is worth singling out the tomb of the Bulls (*c.* 530 BC) belonging to the important Spurinna family. It has three chambers, one of them containing a scene of Achilles' ambush of the young Troilus. The tomb of the Augurs (*c.* 520 BC) has only one chamber, decorated on the back wall with two male figures in ritu-

al attitudes, set on each side of a door. On the remaining walls are scenes of games, including the dramatic one of the *phersu*, a hooded figure defending himself with a stick against the attack of a dog held on a leash and set on him by a bearded man.

A different atmosphere characterizes the

Scene with diver,
Hunting and Fishing Tomb,
510 BC

Hunting and Fishing Tomb (c. 510 BC), where a young man about to dive from a rock is set in a lively landscape with birds in flight and darting fish. However, the scene seems to be linked to a complex symbology of the moment of passage to the hereafter.

Also set in the open air are the pictures in the tomb of the Hunter (510-500 BC), transformed into a spacious tent from which animals can be seen grazing, and in that of the Li-onesses (520 BC), with figures of guests at a banquet lying on patches of grass and watching men and women dancing. The decoration of the tomb of the Baron (510-500 BC) has a solemn appearance, with a rigid alternation of plant motifs with standing and riding figures. One of the best-known painted tombs is undoubtedly that of the Leopards (480-470 BC), named after the figures of felines on the pediment of the rear wall, which has pairs of din-

Scene of game of skill
to the sound of the flute,
tomb of the Jugglers,
second half of the
6th cent. BC

Opposite at top, interior
of the tomb of the Baron,
510-500 BC.; below,
detail of a banqueting
scene, tomb of the
Leopards, 480-470 BC

ers lying on *klinai* and entertained by musicians playing the double flute and the lyre.

In several cases, however, requirements of protection and preservation have made it necessary to transfer the more fragile paintings to the Tarquinia Museum, where it is now possible to see a reconstruction of the tomb of the Triclinium (470-460 BC), perhaps the most famous for the refinement of its composition and colors, as well as the tombs of the Chariots (490 BC), the Olympics (*c.* 520 BC) and the Ship. The name of the latter, dating from around the middle of the 5th cent. BC, alludes to the representation of the perilous voyage to the afterworld aboard a large vessel.

Large numbers of tombs with decorated walls were still built over the following decades, but the serene depictions of everyday life, profoundly imbued with realism, that had been their most evident feature gave way to darker visions, thronged with demons, and scenes of the journey to the next world. These would be repeated in obsessive fashion throughout the 4th and 3rd centuries, in close connection with a more uncertain political situation, when the tombs housed several depositions inside large sarcophagi produced by the still flourishing local craftsmen. From this period dates the extraordinary Orcus Tomb, owned by the Murina family, created out of the union of different tombs in antiquity and famous for its delicate representation of a girl from the Velcha family called Velia in the oldest chamber (350-325 BC), and for its beautifully colored images of mythical heroes and gods of the underworld in the most recent one. It is also worth mentioning the tomb of the Shields (late 4th cent. BC), belonging to the Velcha family, whose aristocratic rank is reflected by the fascinating paintings of the central chamber, with a scene of the deceased departing for the hereafter, and the Giglioli Tomb (3rd cent. BC), with large shields and pieces of armor painted on the walls in a sort of frieze.

At the beginning of the 4th century Tar-

Flautist entertaining the banqueters, tomb of the Leopards, 480-470 BC

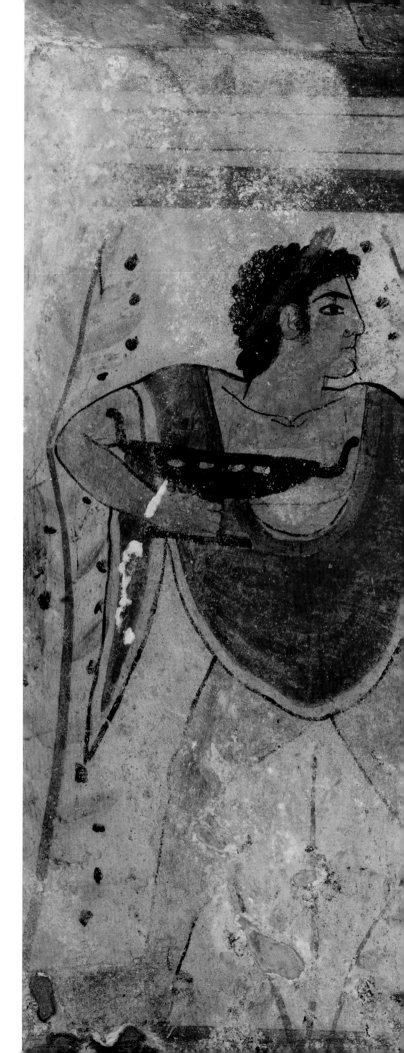

Detail of the face of Velia Velcha in the Orcus Tomb, third quarter of the 4th cent. BC

quinii appears, against the trend in much of the rest of Etruria, to have been a thriving city, capable of controlling a vast hinterland and making its political weight felt in the "Etruscan confederation", i.e. the league of twelve peoples of Etruria that used to meet at the federal sanctuary in Volsinii. This economic growth also found expression in a revival of building activity and Tarquinii was fortified with walls stretching for about 8 km, which followed the contours of the Civita hill and surrounded an area of over 130 hectares.

In this period the political scene in the city and Etruria in general was dominated by Aule Spurinna, a member of one of the local noble families. His exploits, mentioned in the so-called *elogia Tarquiniensia* (an epigraph with celebratory inscriptions from the imperial age), were focused on putting down a slave revolt that had broken out at Arezzo (ancient Arretium), on deposing King Orgolnius of Caere and on opposing the ever growing power of

Rome. His military offensive against Rome (358 and 351 BC) was not crowned with success, although in the second half of the century numerous centers in the territory of Tarquinii underwent a remarkable economic and cultural revival based on an exploitation of agriculture. The end of the century saw the loss of the city's hegemony in the Etruscan League and the opening decades of the 3rd were marked by new clashes with the Romans. In 281 BC the latter succeeded in conquering the great Etruscan city, resulting in the loss of part of its coastal territory and triggering a slow decline of the local aristocracy. Its members were later to seek new fortune in Rome, holding important public posts or placing themselves at the service of the imperial court as repositories of the secrets of haruspicy.

Gravisca (Porto Clementino)

The old port of Tarquinii, whose Etruscan name is unknown, was created at the beginning of the 6th cent. BC to the south of the mouth of the Marta, on what would later be the site of the Roman colony of Gravisca. Only a few parts of the ancient settlement have been uncovered, while greater information has come from the excavation of the sanctuary dating from the Archaic period, which, on the basis of the dedications in Etruscan and Greek, appears to have been consecrated to Turan-Aphrodite. Other deities were venerated there that can be identified with the Greek goddesses Demeter (Vei in Etruscan) and Hera (Uni in Etruscan). The place of worship seems to have been frequented from the outset by Greek merchants from Samos and Miletus, and subsequently by Aeginetans as well, including the celebrated Sostratus, whose memory is preserved by a dedicatory inscription on a stone anchor found at Gravisca (now in the Tarquinia Museum), as well as by Herodotus's reference to the fabulous wealth he accumulated through trade.

The Greek presence appears to have diminished significantly in the decade from 480 to 470 BC, following the continuous clashes that took place in the Tyrrhenian Sea and inevitably brought a slow decline of the port. From this time on, in fact, even visitors to the sanctuary were almost exclusively confined to the local populations. With the end of Tarquinii's independence (281 BC), the port's role became more marginal, until a Roman colony with the name of Gravisca was founded a hundred years later on the same site, although it covered a much smaller area than the earlier settlement. After this period it appeared frequently in the literary sources and was mentioned by Cato, who explained its name by the bad air (*gravem aerem*) of the zone, following the transformation of much of the shoreline into marshland.

Stone anchor with inscription dedicated to Aeginetan Apollo by Sostratus, from Gravisca, late 6th cent. BC. Museo Archeologico Nazionale, Tarquinia

Vulci

The castle of Vulci,
seat of the Archeological
Museum, and the
Etrusco-Roman bridge
of the Badia

Cinerary hut urn in
bronze plate, from Vulci,
mid-8th cent. BC.
Museo Nazionale Etrusco
di Villa Giulia, Rome

The ancient city of Vulci, called Velch by the Etruscans and indicated today by the presence of the solitary castle of Badia, stood in a naturally protected position on a large plateau just over 12 km from the coast.

The important Etruscan settlement was located at the center of a fertile region extending between the valleys of the Fiora and the Albegna, an area that appears to have already been densely populated in pre-Etruscan times. Numerous necropolises (with well, pit and chest tombs) from the Iron Age have been found around the Vulci plateau and seem to suggest a series of separate villages. They have yielded biconical cinerary urns covered by bowls or clay helmets, or hut urns that in some cases, such as the fine example from the necropolis of the Osteria (Museo di Villa Giulia, Rome), are made out of embossed bronze. Objects of foreign origin were already present among the grave goods in this period, demonstrating the existence of extensive trade relations. Among them is the bronze figure of a warrior imported from Sardinia (second half of the 9th cent. BC) that has given the tomb of the Nuraghic Bronze its name. At the end of the 8th century various artifacts from Greece made their appearance, the most interesting of which is the Euboean krater found at Pescia Romana and now in the Grosseto Museum.

The urban center of the city was formed by fusion of the Iron Age villages, but in the Orientalizing period it is again the tombs that offer eloquent testimony to the cultural development of the city and the opulence of the local aristocracy. The tomb of the Bronze Chariot, dated to 680-670 BC, constitutes a record of extraordinary importance owing to its rich contents, relating to the custom of the banquet, which accompanied at least three burials, and the bronze chariot with repoussé decorations from which it takes its name.

Subsequent graves continue to reflect the thriving state of Vulci's economy for the rest of the 7th century. Exemplary of this are the rich materials from the tomb of Isis in the necropolis of La Polledrara: terracotta statuettes of women, flasks, Egyptian scarabs and ostrich eggs with a lavish ornamentation that can be attributed to the sophisticated local craftsmen, like the numerous bronze artifacts found in the same complex. In the final decades of the century there was also a prolific production of pottery based on Greek and in particular Corinthian models, which was accompanied by a series of sculptures in nenfro, many of them representing fantastic animals

like the well-known statues of a centaur and of a youth astride a sea monster, both in the Museo di Villa Giulia. These sculptures were the first in a series that was to influence the output of many other centers for several decades, even in inland Northern Etruria.

The tomb architecture of Vulci, on the other hand, is characterized by modest constructions, which contrast with the large burial mounds of the Orientalizing period. Some of these, such as the monumental Cuccumella in the necropolis of Cavalupo, are richly decorated.

The city's extensive maritime trade was conducted through several landing places on the coast, including the mouth of the Fiora and above all the port of Regisvilla (at the locality of Morelle), where the remains of a settlement that developed along the roads linking it to Vulci have been brought to light. A large building has also been discovered that was used in the second half of the 6th cent. BC and contained quantities of pottery that once again underline the intense level of trade with the Greek world and other parts of the Mediterranean. Remains from the later Etruscan and

Pontic pottery, from Vulci, second half of the 6th cent. BC. Museo Nazionale Etrusco di Villa Giulia, Rome

Euboean krater by the Cesnola Painter, from Pescia Romana, 730-720 BC. Museo Archeologico e d'Arte della Maremma, Grosseto

Statues of women from the tomb at La Polledrara, Vulci, 570-560 BC. British Museum, London

Centaur from the necropolis of Poggio Maremma, Vulci, early 6th cent. BC. Museo Nazionale Etrusco di Villa Giulia, Rome

Roman periods are known from the same locality, including the harbor and a villa.

In the 6th century and the early decades of the 5th, Vulci still appears to have been a very active center, maintaining its dominance of the import of Attic pottery but simultaneously developing its own production of vases in the same style, which were sold not only to local customers but also to other Etruscan cities.

As in the other coastal cities of Southern Etruria, the defeat of the Etruscan fleet at the battle of Cumae (474 BC) brought economic activity to an abrupt standstill in Vulci, placing severe limits on maritime trade. The city reacted by shifting the focus of its attention to agricultural exploitation of the fertile territory, documented by the resurgence of minor settlements that would contribute to a renewed prosperity right through the 4th century and

up until the early decades of the 3rd. This is the period (second half of the 4th cent.) from which dates the François Tomb in the necropolis of Ponte Rotto, belonging to the aristocratic Saties family. It consists of a long *dromos* leading to a cross-shaped room onto which open seven symmetrical chambers decorated with an extraordinary cycle of paintings: detached in the 19th century, they are now in a private collection. Representing duels between heroes of Vulci and adversaries from Rome, Volsinii, Falerii and Suana (now Sovana), they refer to legendary episodes that were supposed to have occurred in the 6th century, but brought up to date by their relevance to the contemporary struggles between the Etruscan city and Rome.

Vulci appears only rarely in the literary sources, but the defeat inflicted on it and Volsinii in 280 BC by Titus Coruncanius is mentioned in the *Capitoline fasti*. The ensuing expropriation of vast plots of land marked the beginning of the city's slow decline, a process that was accelerated by the foundation of the Roman colony of Cosa in 273 BC.

Opposite, youth astride a sea monster from the necropolis of Poggio Maremma, Vulci, mid-6th cent. BC. Museo Nazionale Etrusco di Villa Giulia, Rome

Cosa (Ansedonia)

View of the remains
of the Capitolium on
the acropolis of Cosa

Cosa was constructed by the Romans in 273 BC, seven years after the victory over Vulci, with the aim of exercising control over the recently conquered territory.

The city stood in an elevated position, on a promontory sheer above the sea, and occupied an area of 13 hectares. It was ringed by walls in *opus siliceum* that stretched for 1.5 km and were equipped with nineteen towers and three gates leading respectively to Porto Ercole, the Via Aurelia below and the city's harbor. It was laid out in the traditional Roman grid of streets oriented according to the points of the compass (*decumani* running from east to west, *cardines* from north to south). The forum housed the city's public buildings (*curia, comitia, basilica*), where commercial and political activities were carried out in imitation of the one in Rome. The sacred buildings were located in the highest part of the city, the acropolis (*arx*), defended by its own ring of walls with two gates. In this zone can be seen the majestic remains of the Capitolium (150 BC) dedicated to Jupiter-Juno-Minerva, built on the site of a previous place of worship. It had a sumptuous decoration of terracotta slabs that are now on display in the local museum, situated in the area of the ancient city. Huge dwellings have been excavated in the urban area, including

that of the Skeleton, which got its name from the discovery of a skeleton in the cistern underneath, built at the beginning of the 1st cent. BC. The city was connected with its port (Portus Cosanus), of which some imposing structures have survived, along with the so-called Tagliata or "Cutting," a canal almost 100 m long that runs partly in the open and partly through a tunnel to provide a link between the open sea and the lagoon.

Near the beach of the Tagliata can be seen the ruins of a large villa with a system for the raising of fish. Luxurious residences of this kind are present in other parts of the former territory of Cosa, including those of the Colonne, which takes its name from the monumental enclosure studded with large columns, and of Settefinestre. (G.P.)

Remains of port
structures on the coast
at Cosa-Ansedonia

Opposite, a view of
the canal at Cosa called
the *Tagliata Etrusca*
("Etruscan Cutting")

The Production of Bucchero

I *Bucchero* was undoubtedly the type of pottery most characteristic of Etruscan civilization, to the point where it has become a symbol of it. In antiquity its popularity extended beyond the confines of the Italian peninsula, taking it all over the Mediterranean and even into Central Europe.

Typically black on both the outside and inside, as well as light and shiny, *bucchero* ware is in reality the heir of a very long prehistoric and protohistoric tradition, although it first appeared in Caere in the 7th cent. BC. In fact the peoples of the Bronze Age already used to mold containers by hand out of a crude mixture of clay and fillers (sand, crushed stone), polishing the exterior

with sticks before firing them. Once they had been fired in primitive and poorly ventilated kilns, similar to charcoal piles, these pots acquired a translucent but irregular blackish-brown coloring.

It was the potters of Caere (modern Cerveteri) who, in an attempt to imitate metal ware, developed a special method of firing to produce ceramics of a uniformly black color. The object, thrown from clay (although some have suggested the addition of special substances, such as manganese or organic products), was polished before firing, decorated with engravings, stamped impressions or applications and left to dry in the air. It was the subsequent firing that gave the pots their characteristic color; while for ordinary objects in reddish earthenware, the kilns were kept open so that the influx of air permitted a rapid and complete oxidation of the chemical components of the vase, to make *bucchero* ware the kilns were closed so that the pots were slowly "carbonized" in the absence of oxygen. After firing, the piece was polished further while still hot.

The oldest *bucchero* has extremely thin walls, but from the 6th century onward so-called *bucchero pesante* was introduced, characterized by thick walls covered with ornaments in relief in

Above, Orientalizing pyx with bull's heads. Museo Gregoriano Etrusco, Vatican

Above, amphora with cylinder decoration, from Sarteano, early 6th cent. BC. Sarteano, Museo Civico Archeologico

imitation of contemporary metal containers with *repoussé* decoration. This variant, produced with particular success by the potteries of Clusium (Chiusi), is roughly contemporary with *bucchero grigio*, a ware that presents an ash-gray color both on the surface and when broken, which was particularly widespread in inland Northern Etruria.

With the passage of time, however, the production of *bucchero* ware became more shoddy and was marginalized to a few markets (5th cent. BC), losing the elegance of form and ornamentation that had initially distinguished it as a product of quality intended for the upper classes.

The *bucchero* technique was used to produce pots of many different shapes,

Goblet from Falerii Veteres, mid-7th cent. BC; right, *oinochoe* from Ischia di Castro, late 7th cent. BC. Museo Nazionale Etrusco di Villa Giulia, Rome

Above, *kotyle* from tomb II of the Montetosto Tumulus at Cerveteri, third quarter of the 7th cent. BC. Museo Nazionale Etrusco di Villa Giulia, Rome

Above, *oinochoe* **in** *bucchero pesante,* **6th cent. BC. Museo Archeologico, Florence**

Above right, bowl from the tomb of the Painted Lions, Banditaccia Necropolis at Cerveteri, first half of the 6th cent. BC. Museo Nazionale Etrusco di Villa Giulia, Rome

used mainly for cooking and the table. Various vessels, such as bowls, dishes, and plates, were utilized for the consumption of food and were kept hot, when necessary, by placing them inside braziers or *foculi.* Also made of *bucchero,* these were a typical product of Clusium.

The ceremony of the symposium also entailed extensive use of *bucchero* ware for serving the drinks. The wine was brought in amphorae to the table, where it was poured into kraters by slaves and mixed with water stored in a *hydria* (a rounded vase with three handles: two for carrying, one for pouring). From the kraters, characterized by large mouths and rounded bellies, the drink was often strained to remove the herbs that had been added to ensure its preservation and enrich its flavor. These operations

were carried out with special dippers and strainers, and then the drink was poured into jugs of various kinds (*oinochoai, olpai*), sometimes in the shape of animals (*askoi*). Cups with tall stems and no handles were used for drinking. In the oldest examples made of *bucchero* these were sometimes supported by small openwork figures called caryatids. Alternatively the wine was served in *kyathoi* (goblets with a low stem and a single, raised handle) or *kantharoi* (similar to the former but with two handles). Following the Greek fashion, the *kylix* was also introduced: a low and wide-mouthed drinking cup with slender horizontal handles and a high foot, it was indispensable for the game of *cottabus,* in which guests had to bring down a metal disk balanced on a slender support by throwing wine at it from their cups.

Foculus **from Chiusi, second half of the 6th cent. BC. Chiusi, Museo Archeologico Nazionale**

Bucchero was also used to make *alabastra* and *aryballoi,* small pots used to hold perfumes and essences, or pyxes, small cylindrical containers for cosmetics and jewels, as well as incense burners on tall stems or *situlae* and small buckets. (M.M.)

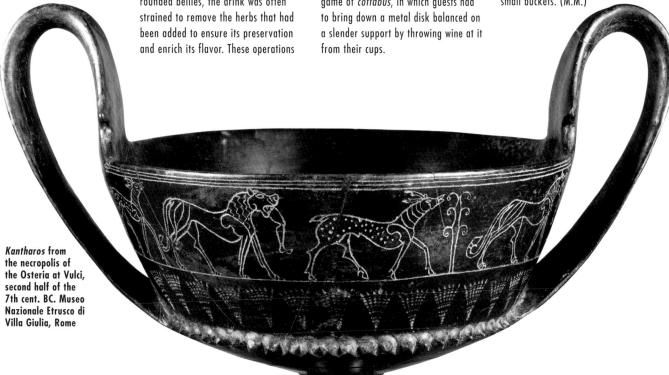

Kantharos **from the necropolis of the Osteria at Vulci, second half of the 7th cent. BC. Museo Nazionale Etrusco di Villa Giulia, Rome**

Religion

The religious beliefs of the Etruscans underwent continual evolution, in step with the various phases of their civilization. In the early Iron Age they took the primitive form of an animistic veneration of abstract principles or natural elements such as springs, forces of nature, aspects of the plant world or totemic animals.

A telling example of the worship of an abstract principle governing nature is

Hellenistic era Velthumna (*deus Etruriae princeps*) was venerated at the sanctuary of Volsinii, where the twelve main cities of the Etruscan League held their annual assemblies.

Endless examples of cults linked to water have been documented in Etruria, from the spring sanctuary of San Giovenale to the stalactites of Grotta Lattaia in the province of Siena and the sacred complex of the hot springs at

been found at San Giovenale, for example, where sacred feasts were held periodically in a hut in the vicinity of the source of spring water, while the lid of the cinerary urn from the Olmo Bello at Bisenzio – late 8th cent. BC – seems to represent a collective rite, in which armed men perform a dance in the presence of a totemic animal, ringed by two circles of dancers.

Apparent order was brought to this confused jumble of magic and animism – combined, moreover, with traditional ancestor worship – by the influence of Hellenic culture. During the 7th century, this introduced a "rational" Olympic pantheon of gods and goddesses with a humanized appearance. And yet the gods that were defined as equivalents of the Greek (or sometimes Phoenician) deities in Etruria very often retained a number of aspects of more primitive divinities. The most important deity of the new pantheon, Tinia, gave human beings the very concept of the boundary, so as to impart order to their world in the image of the more rational one of the gods; and thus made it possible for them to separate as well, to eliminate uncertainties and conflicts, to fix with objectivity everything that exists.

With his subdivision of the cosmos, therefore, Tinia made it known that there were various *sedes deorum* in the heavenly sphere, i.e. spaces assigned to each deity. These formed the *templum*, the whole of the universe based on a fixed module. Its conformation applied to celestial space (the *templum maius*) was the one recorded by Pliny in his *Natural History*, where he stated that the whole of space was divided by a cross formed by the *cardo* – the line linking the north with the south – and the *decumanus*, the line at right angles uniting east and west. Each of the four quadrants obtained in this way was made up of four sectors, producing a total of sixteen areas of the *templum*, each the seat of a particular deity. The same module was repeated in microcosms and macrocosms that were all alike and contained one inside the other, present in every area defined as

provided by the god Velthumna (Vertumnus for the Latins), venerated from prehistoric until Roman times in a guise that was essentially devoid of precise characteristics. Incarnating the principle of the regeneration and perpetual transformation of nature by which "nothing is created and everything is transformed," his cult was maintained for the entire duration of Etruscan civilization, and in the

Sasso Pisano. This aspect of popular Etruscan religiosity has even survived into our own day, as is testified by the many pilgrims who still flock to churches built near miraculous springs. A number of animals, such as stags, also performed a totemic function and were probably the object of ritual or initiatory hunts, after which they were consumed by the whole community. Remains of bones and antlers have

Setting of ring with scene of worship in front of a fountain, from Cerveteri, last quarter of the 6th cent. BC.
Museo Nazionale Etrusco di Villa Giulia, Rome

Detail of the lid of a cinerary urn from the Olmo Bello Necropolis at Bisenzio, late 8th cent. BC.
Museo Nazionale Etrusco di Villa Giulia, Rome

Top, small bronze representing Minerva, 475-450 BC. Galleria Estense, Modena; above, small bronze representing a haruspex with a *lituus* from Isola di Fano near Fossombrone, 480 BC. Museo Archeologico, Florence

Lid of the cinerary urn of the priest Aule Lecu, represented in the act of examining a liver, late 2nd-early 1st cent. BC. Museo Guarnacci, Volterra

Below, bronze model of liver indicating the seats of the deities, from Decima, Piacenza, 2nd cent. BC. Museo Civico, Piacenza

sacred. Given that the priests were able to delimit a sacred area anywhere with a gesture of the *lituus* (the curved sacred staff once an attribute of shepherds and which has now become the pastoral staff carried by bishops), or just of their fingers over the viscera of animals, every area or space, undergoing the sacred delimitation called *limitatio*, revealed its hidden essence of *templum*. Thus each deity sent its signs from its own seat in the sector, identified and defined by the priest: a *templum* extended over cities, for the interpretation of lightning bolts and the flight of birds; a *templum* lay above the liver of sacrificial victims, and many other *templa* could be defined in every part of real space, making it possible — as if in a magic mirror — to see the divine will of the moment reflected in it. With the introduction of the principle of "dividing in order to understand" into a world where the ownership of land and geographical exploration were spreading, the action of human beings on their surroundings was symbolically legitimized by the gods, who gave the instrument of rational cognition to the Etruscan people.

According to Cicero (*De divinatione*), the definition of this scheme, as well as the ability to interpret and apply it, had been the subject of a further revelation by the gods. A mythical figure called Tages had communicated the elements of the sacred and civil division of space and land to a multitude of people who gathered on his sudden appearance from a furrow in the ground in the vicinity of Tarquinii. As time passed these notions were added to and came to form a doctrine, but the underlying principles would remain the ones indicated by Tages. The interpretation of the hidden meaning of what happened in everyday life, in the light of divine revelation, was a distinctive feature of Etruscan civilization, and made the ideology and sensibility of this people deeply fatalistic, quite unlike those of any other contemporary ethnic group. With this perception of reality, every human action in the world had to be evaluated in relation to the gods, even before it was carried out, so as not to run the risk of being involuntarily disrespectful to them and incurring their anger. This amounted, in the words of Massimo Pallottino, to "an abandonment, almost an abdication of human spiritual activity before divinity: which was revealed in the twofold obsession with understanding and carrying out the divine will." It was this spirit that gave rise, in the

Mirror with Calchas examining a liver, 4th cent. BC. Museo Gregoriano Etrusco, Vatican

later phases of Etruscan culture, to a widespread anxiety about a hereafter where the individual's life and ability to respect the divine would be subject to severe judgment. To this peculiar characteristic were added the effects of the diffusion of Dionysian ideas, mystery cults and rituals for the salvation of souls from the Eastern Mediterranean. These gained ground in the rest of the Italian peninsula as well, leading — as in Rome — to harsh repressive measures in defense of traditional religion. While the gloomy atmosphere of the funereal world of later periods is widely documented in the art of the Hellenistic period, the votive cult that was practiced in the temples appears to have been much more lively: the temples drew ever greater numbers of people at a time when, according to a prophecy, the Etruscan civilization was on the point of fulfilling its destiny, fated to last for ten *saecula*. (M.M.)

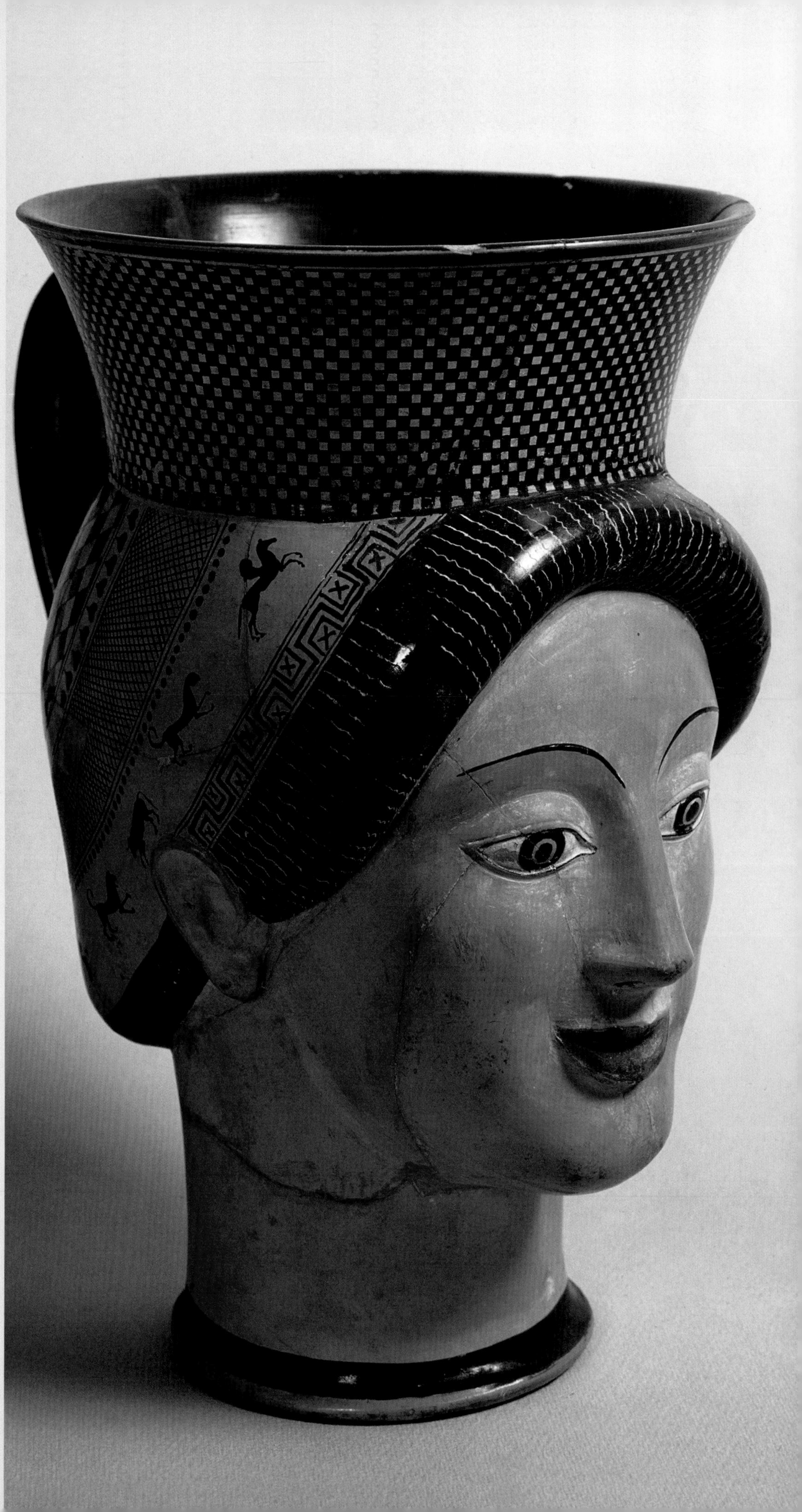

Palazzo Vitelleschi, seat of the Museo Archeologico Nazionale

Opposite, *rhyton* **made in Attica attributed to Charinos, from Tarquinii, early 5th cent. BC**

The museum is located in one of the most interesting 15th-century buildings in Lazio, built by Cardinal Vitelleschi and used for a variety of purposes over the centuries. After the decision to turn it into a museum at the beginning of the last century, it was inaugurated in 1924 with the pieces in the municipal collection and the large Bruschi-Falgari collection that had been acquired by the State. Over the years it has been enriched with materials from excavations carried out in the region and is now one of the most important museums of Etruscan antiquities. The oldest phase of the Etruscan city is represented by numerous artifacts of

Villanovan culture (9th-8th cent. BC) found in pit tombs or stone chests, attesting to the absolute predominance of the rite of cremation. The ossuaries are of the biconical type, covered with a bowl or a bronze helmet. More rare are the small urns in the shape of huts, which provide important clues to the appearance of Iron-Age dwellings. Some of the graves contained *impasto* models of carts and ships reflecting the activities pursued by the deceased. The famous chamber Tomb of Bocchoris can be dated to the beginning of the

Above right, incense-burner cart from the Monterozzi Necropolis at Tarquinia, first quarter of the 8th cent. BC

Impasto hut urn from the Monterozzi Necropolis at Tarquinia, 8th cent. BC

Situla **in glazed terracotta made in Egypt from the tomb of Bocchoris, last quarter of the 8th cent. BC**

Trumpet called a *lituus* **from the sacred area of La Civita at Tarquinia, second half of the 8th cent. BC**

Orientalizing period and takes its name from the inscription on a faience vase, in Egyptian hieroglyphics, citing the pharaoh of the 24th dynasty who reigned from 720 to 712 BC. More or less contemporary are some grave goods from the necropolis of Monterozzi, including the particularly sumptuous contents of the tomb of the Gold Pectoral. These comprise finely decorated ostrich eggs, objects carved from ivory and the breastplate that gives the grave its name, made at a local workshop in which craftsmen of Oriental origin operated. Another rich deposit comes from Poggio Gallinaro and consists of objects in *bucchero* reproducing the two-edged ax, a symbol of the power attained by the deceased. Also on display in the museum are the important finds recently brought to light in the votive deposit of the sacred complex at La Civita, which include several objects of high religious value, such as a kind of trumpet called a *lituus*, an ax and a bronze shield.

The prosperity attained by Tarquinii over the course of the 7th and 6th century is amply testified by the extensive collection of pottery, arranged by category since the original context of provenance is unknown. There are large numbers of vessels produced in Corinth and imitations made by local potteries, in addition to those imported from Eastern Greece and, in particular, ointment jars of various forms. Representing animals and parts of the human body, such as legs and helmed heads, these must have held unguents of foreign manufacture. Also of great significance is the collection of *bucchero* vases stamped with designs produced by molds and rolling with cylinders, and of black-figure pottery produced in Athens by the greatest painters of the time and acquired by the local aristocracy during

the 6th century. The high quality of such imports is also reflected by the red-figure pottery, which includes a krater decorated by the Berlin Painter (500-490 BC) with an image of Europa and the bull. A large *amphora* representing the struggle between Apollo and Heracles for the tripod was executed by Pinthias (520-510 BC), who has proudly set his name on the work, as have the potter Euxitheos and the painter Oltos on a goblet of monumental dimensions (510-500 BC), decorated on the inside with a running warrior and on the outside with a complicated scene consisting of an assembly of gods and Dionysus on his

Above, Attic krater attributed to the Berlin Painter, from Tarquinii, 500-490 BC; above, black-figure amphora attributed to the Micali Painter

Kylix attributed to Oltos, from Tarquinia, 510-500 BC.

chariot with his retinue of revelers. The impressive vase has a dedication to the Dioscuri in Etruscan on the foot. Another vase of great visual effect is the one in the shape of a woman's head bearing the signature of the potter Charinos, active at the beginning of the 5th cent. BC. The majestic terracotta winged horses dating from the beginning of the 4th cent. BC used to adorn the monumental sanctuary of the Ara della Regina ("Altar of the Queen"), which stood on the plateau of La Civita. The collection of stone sarcophagi found in the tombs of the most well-to-do families of Tarquinii from the 4th cent. BC onward is extensive and of high quality. Among the oldest examples, the one known as the sarcophagus of the "priest," has the recumbent figure of the deceased head of the Partunu family on the lid. It was carved in Greece out of prized Parian marble, while the chest is adorned with a decoration painted by a local craftsman that is intended to represent the killing of Trojan prisoners on the grave of Patroclus. The sarcophagus of the "magnate," carved out of white limestone by skilled sculptors from Tarquinii, with a rich zoomorphic decoration at the end of the bolster, must have belonged to another member of the same family who died at the age of 82 after having held the post of magistrate in the Etruscan city. The chest is decorated on all four sides with scenes of battle against the Amazons and the Centaurs. Another particularly

important personage in the Tarquinii of the first half of the 3rd century was Laris Pulena, interred in the sarcophagus of the "magistrate." He is depicted in heroic semi-nudity and holds a scroll with a long inscription in Etruscan recording his Greek origins, his special devotion to the deities Catha and Pacha and the important public posts he held in his life, as well as a number of sacred texts. The chest is decorated with a scene connected with

Above, "Sarcophagus of the Priest" from the tomb of the Partunu, 360-350 BC.; above, "Sarcophagus of the Magnate" from the tomb of the Partunu, third quarter of the 4th cent. BC

Opposite, the Winged Horses from the sanctuary of the Ara della Regina at Tarquinia, early 4th cent. BC

the afterworld, peopled by Etruscan demons of death. Representations of the journey into the afterlife also appear on some sarcophagi of the Camna family.

The visit concludes with the reconstruction of several tombs with wall paintings (tomb of the Chariots, tomb of the *Triclinium*, tomb of the Ship, tomb of the Olympics) that were detached and moved to the museum, along with the Bruschi Tomb and the tomb of the Black Sow, which are not on display. (G.P.)

The Museo Nazionale Etrusco di Villa Giulia

The Etruscan Museum was set up in 1889 and is located in the picturesque residence built for Pope Julius III by Jacopo Vignola in the middle of the 16th century, in collaboration with Giorgio Vasari and Bartolommeo Ammannati. Initially intended to house pre-Roman antiquities from Latium, it was later enriched with Etruscan artifacts found in campaigns of excavation or acquired on the market and is now one of the most representative of the museums devoted to Etruscan civilization.

The exhibits are arranged according to topographical criteria, with the

Small bronze of Sardinian make from the Cavalupo Necropolis at Vulci, 9th cent. BC

presentation of exceptional groups of finds from the wealthy cities of Southern Etruria, as well as Umbria, Sabina and Latium Vetus. There are also pieces of extraordinary value in the Antiquarium, most of them from the Museo Kircheriano and the rich Cima Pesciotti and Castellani collections.

Five of the museum's rooms are devoted to the city of Vulci, whose extensive cemeteries have yielded such interesting finds as the biconical ossuaries with helmet-shaped lids and hut-shaped urns (9th-8th cent. BC) from the necropolises at Mandrione di Cavalupo. It is worth singling out the contents of the tomb of the Nuraghic Bronze (second half of the 9th cent. BC), belonging to a woman of high rank. They include bronze statuettes of Sardinian production (among them a small figure with a tall headdress and large shield) that bear witness to the

Above, large amphora attributed to the Painter of the Bearded Sphinx, from the necropolis of the Osteria at Vulci, late 7th cent. BC

Bronze plaque representing Achilles's attack on Troilus, from the necropolis of the Osteria at Vulci, second half of the 6th cent. BC

antiquity of trade between Vulci and the island. Other materials from the Villanovan period come from the cemeteries of the Osteria, including a hut urn in laminated bronze dating from the first half of the 8th cent. BC, and the extraordinary objects from the tomb of the Bronze Chariot (680-670 BC). Discovered intact with at least three graves and a large collection of bronze and *impasto* vessels, it also contained a chariot covered with embossed sheets of bronze. This must have originally carried a schematic human figure, about to set off on the journey into the hereafter. Also from the cemeteries of the Osteria comes the tomb of the Warrior (*c.* 520 BC), containing the complete bronze armor of a hoplite, including a pair of embossed plates representing Achilles's ambush of Troilus at a fountain. Among the rich contents of the grave were also pottery from Greece and bronze vessels that demonstrate the refinement achieved by the craftsmen of Vulci, well documented by a basin adorned on the lip with figures of lions.

The other rooms dedicated to Vulci house numerous examples of Etrusco-Corinthian pottery produced in local

workshops, including several decorated by the Painter of the Bearded Sphinx (closing decades of the 7th cent. BC), and some sculptures in nenfro, such as the famous *Centaur* and the *Youth on a Sea Horse* (6th cent. BC), uncovered in the necropolises at Poggio Maremma. From the territory of Vulci also comes a two-horse chariot with refined decorations in bronze, excavated from a tomb discovered near Castro in 1967 that belonged to a personage of rank who died in the last decades of the 6th century.

The ancient city Bisentium or Visentium (modern Bisenzio), and especially the necropolis of Olmo Bello, has yielded grave goods of extraordinary interest. Numerous *impasto* pots, hut urns and locally produced ceramics with geometric decorations testify to the flowering of the settlement on the western shore of Lake Bolsena from the 9th cent. BC onward. Of particular importance are a ceremonial cart from the second half of the 8th century adorned with various groups of statuettes and an amphora made of bronze plate, datable to 730-700 BC, whose lid is decorated with seven figures dancing around a monstrous

Amphora in bronze plate and, below, *bullae* in gold foil from tomb II, necropolis of the Olmo Bello at Bisenzio, second half of the 8th cent. BC

creature that can be identified as a god of the underworld.

The rooms devoted to Veii contain the famous statues that used to stand on the roof of the sanctuary at Portonaccio, representing the contest between *Apollo and Heracles for Possession of the Ceryneian Hind* with its golden horns. Watching the hero engaged in his labor are *Leto Holding the Baby Apollo* and *Hermes*, masterpieces of Etruscan ceramics of the late 6th cent. BC, a period when Veii was home to one of the most important and refined workshops for the production of terracotta figures, run by Vulca. The great master, formerly thought to have made the most significant of the statues, was also summoned to nearby Rome to adorn the temple of Capitoline Jupiter with his creations.

A reconstruction of the Maroi Tomb, discovered in the cemetery of the Banditaccia, introduces the vast collection of objects from Caere. The

materials on display underline the importance and wealth of the Etruscan city, with its imposing places of worship and huge graveyards with monumental tumuli.

Some of the oldest finds, datable to between the 9th and 8th cent. BC, come from the necropolises of the Cava della Pozzolana and Sorbo, but it is the celebrated *Sarcophagus of the Married Couple* (6th cent. BC) from the Banditaccia that grabs attention. It represents a husband and his wife reclining on a *kline* at a banquet: the half-naked man is embracing his companion, who wears a long chiton under a cloak, the typical Etruscan

Head of Hermes from the sanctuary of Portonaccio at Veio, late 6th cent. BC

Terracotta group with Leto and the baby Apollo from the sanctuary of Portonaccio at Veio, late 6th cent. BC

Above right, terracotta sarcophagus with felines from Procoio di Ceri, mid-6th cent. BC; below, lid of cinerary urn with married couple, from the Banditaccia Necropolis at Cerveteri, second half of the 6th cent. BC

Below, the "Sarcophagus of the Married Couple" from the Banditaccia Necropolis at Cerveteri, second half of the 6th cent. BC; following pages, a detail

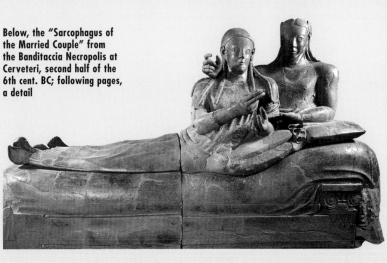

headdress known as a *tutulus* and pointed shoes.

Further evidence of Caere's wealth is provided by the contents of the tomb of the Firedogs and the tumulus of the Ship, which comprise some important specimens of Greek pottery, including a krater from Corinth with warriors on horseback and chariots. From other graves come *bucchero* ware, Laconian ceramics representing the myth of Achilles and Troilus and several *hydriai* with scenes of the combat between Heracles and the centaur Nessus and the blinding of Polyphemus. They were produced for a refined clientele by craftsmen of North Ionian origin who settled in Caere in the second half of the 6th cent. BC.

The "Plowman of Arezzo," late 5th cent. BC.; below, gold fibula with Chimera from Cerveteri, second half of the 6th cent. BC

The material from the sanctuary at Pyrgi, Caere's port, is displayed in the room of Venus: along with the high relief representing the myth of the *Seven against Thebes* that adorned the rear end of Temple A (460-450 BC) and numerous architectural decorations from the parallel Temple B (*c.* 500 BC), there are gold leaf tablets with dedications in Etruscan and Phoenician made by the king of Caere, Thefarie Velianas, to Uni-Astarte, the goddess venerated at the shrine.

The extensive range of wall paintings from Tarquinii, finally, is represented by the reconstruction of the tomb of the Funeral Bed (*c.* 460 BC). It consists of a single chamber adorned on the back wall with a large decorated bed on which are set two "headdresses"; most of the other scenes extol the memory of the deceased with figures of diners and athletic contests accompanied by musicians. Now we come to the Antiquarium, housing artifacts of varied provenance that belonged to old collections. Outstanding among the objects in bronze are the well-known *Ficoroni Cist* (4th cent. BC), made by Novios Plautios, which must have contained the toilet articles of a rich matron of Praeneste and is adorned with an episode from the story of the Argonauts, and the *Plowman of*

Arezzo (named after the place it was found), representing a farmer with a pair of oxen and plow. The most significant of the ceramic works is the *Chigi Olpe*: found at Veii, it is decorated on several rows and in vivid colors with the *Judgment of Paris*, hunting scenes and groups of warriors fighting one another with spears and large shields.

The villa's hemicycle houses the prestigious collection of Augusto Castellani, organized into types of material on a chronological basis. There is no room here to describe the large quantity of *bucchero* ware and other pottery present, including works of great refinement made in Athens by such celebrated potters as Lydos, Exekias, Nearchos and Nikosthenes. The goldsmithing skills of members of the Castellani family are amply documented by 19th-century products of their workshop, which are flanked by an extraordinary collection of ancient gold work dating from between the Orientalizing period and the early Middle Ages.

The recent rearrangement of the Faliscan collections in several rooms makes a considerable contribution to a better understanding of the ancient civilization that emerged in the mid-valley of the Tiber. Tombs in the main centers, Narce, Capena and Falerii Veteres, have yielded finds of undoubted interest, in particular

Throne in bronze plate from the Barberini Tomb at Praeneste, first half of the 7th cent. BC

Krater with volutes representing Aurora, from the necropolis of the Colonnette at Falerii Veteres, first half of the 4th cent. BC

Below, *Chigi Olpe* from Veii, second half of the 7th cent. BC

the decoration of the five urban and suburban sanctuaries of Falerii which constitutes one of the most significant relics of the pre-Roman era. From the sanctuary discovered at the locality of Lo Scasato, for example, comes the famous bust of Apollo that was once part of the great high relief on the pediment, dating from the late 4th-early 3rd cent. BC. Even such a rapid survey of the museum cannot leave out the finds from Palestrina, the ancient Latin city of Praeneste. The graves excavated in the middle of the 19th century, i.e. the Barberini and Bernardini tombs, contained objects of extraordinary quality for the Orientalizing period that have no parallel anywhere else in Latium and are comparable only to those of the Regolini-Galassi Tomb in Caere. (G.P.)

Bronze mirror from Praeneste, formerly in the Barberini Collection, late 4th-early 3rd cent. BC

The "Ficoroni Cist" from the necropolis at Palestrina, second half of the 4th cent. BC

Bust of Apollo from the sanctuary of Lo Scasato at Civita Castellana, second half of the 4th cent. BC

Detail of the silver-gilt *patera* of Oriental make, from the Bernardini Tomb at Praeneste, first half of the 7th cent. BC

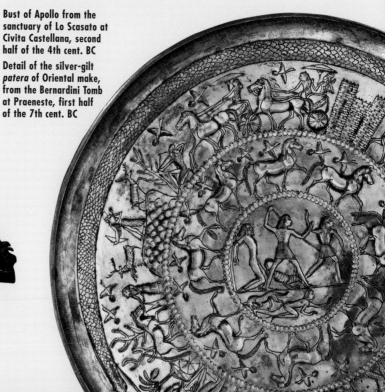

THE UPPER VALLEY OF THE TIBER, VEII AND LAKE BOLSENA

The Faliscan Region, Capena and Lucus Feroniae

The course of the River Tiber has played an important role ever since prehistoric times, simultaneously one of union and division. In fact it has constituted a natural barrier, and thus its opposite banks have often been occupied by different ethnic or political entities; at the same time, given its considerable length, it has served as a means of communication between the inland regions and the areas at its mouth, inhabited by different populations.

The territory situated on its right bank and comprised between the Lake of Bracciano and the Sabatini Mountains, Vico Lake and the Cimini Mountains, was occupied in the Iron Age by the Falisci, a people of Italic stock who came to form a sort of "buffer" between the Etruscans, the Sabines and the peoples of the Adriatic region. Their distinctive character was clear to the ancients themselves. Strabo described the Falisci as "a special and distinct tribe [...] with a special language all its own," despite the fact that the influence of the powerful Etruscan cities in the zone had shaped the culture of the Faliscan centers – Falerii, Narce and Capena – since the 8th century, to such an extent that the latter was called a colony of Veii in the Latin literary sources.

In the Bronze Age the area had been occupied by small, scattered settlements of the rural type, gravitating around Narce but lacking any particular economic or cultural spark. This characteristic diffuse pattern of settlement lasted until around the middle of the 8th cent. BC, when the three main centers began to emerge. In addition to the clear influence of Veii, these showed signs of close contact with the other Italic populations of the area.

The oldest traces of Capena demonstrate that it was initially the dominant Faliscan center, surrounded by minor satellites. The local cemeteries have yielded typical materials like flared cups and disks of armor, which were also common among the Sabini, Piceni, Marrucini, Marsi and Vestini. Equally characteristic are the brown pots with engraved decorations and the cauldrons of reddish *impasto* for dining, set on tall openwork feet and influ-

View of Vico Lake in the Cimini Mountains

Opposite, detail of the head of Hermes from the sanctuary of Portonaccio at Veio, late 6th cent. BC. Museo Nazionale Etrusco di Villa Giulia, Rome

Impasto *kantharos* from the necropolis of San Martino at Capena, second half of the 7th cent. BC. Museo Nazionale Etrusco di Villa Giulia, Rome

From the top, Lararium with mosaics, walls in *opus reticolatum* and peristyle of the villa of the Volusii at Lucus Feroniae

enced by materials imported from the East. The grave goods of the 8th and 7th century reflect a growing prosperity throughout the area, accompanied by a shift from well tombs for cremations to pit tombs for inhumations. These in turn gave way to chamber tombs, which soon became, at Narce for instance, the most common.

The role of hinge played by the Faliscan territory is attested by the stylistic influences conveyed by the materials that arrived, through Veii, from Campania and Southern Latium, and by those discernable in the vessels with plastic figurations derived from Veii and Vulci. While *bucchero* appears initially to have been scarce at Capena, bronze artifacts from the Orientalizing period are present and are comparable with finds made at Praeneste and Caere, and the script, judging by particular features of the inscriptions, may also have been introduced from Caere.

The rapid growth in imports from Corinth, Etruria, Latium and Campania shows that the road system of the region was increasingly being exploited for trade, in an east-west direction as well as along the valley of the Tiber. It is in this context that we should also see the presence of the sanctuary of Feronia in Capena, already flourishing in the 6th cent. BC and located at the intersection of the main routes: according to Livy it was in the local sacred grove (Lucus Feroniae) that the Sabines had seized a number of Roman merchants, during

the reign of Tullus Hostilius, sparking off a war between the two peoples. The sanctuary of this Italic deity, venerated at various places in Latium as the goddess of fertility, harvests and health, attracted large numbers of pilgrims and merchants, who went there for specific festivals. Sacked by Hannibal in 211 BC and then reconstructed, all that remains are the vestiges of walls and an altar in the area of the Roman forum. It was originally the location of the college of the priests called *hirpi* ("wolves"), who carried out ceremonies in the nearby sacred grove, including the rite of walking on burning coals. The numerous votive offerings were not just made out of gratitude for healing, but also to promote the fertility of animals and fields, or the salubrity of waters. In addition, Feronia's role as the protectress of slaves made the sanctuary the theater of ceremonies of "manumission" or "emancipation," i.e. formal liberation from slavery. Enlarged in the Roman era and abandoned in the Middle Ages, it is now open to the public, along with the many structures that have been brought to light, including baths fed by the Aqua Augusta aqueduct and the remains of places of worship.

In the vicinity stand the ruins of the Roman villa that belonged to the Volusii Saturnini (1st cent. BC), while the local museum displays materials from the excavations of the ancient city and from the tombs in its environs.

Falerii (Civita Castellana)

Tuff container with cinerary urn from Falerii Veteres, 8th cent. BC. Museo Nazionale Etrusco di Villa Giulia, Rome

Olla on stand from the necropolis of Le Macchie at Civita Castellana, second half of the 7th cent. BC. Museo Archeologico dell'Agro Falisco, Civita Castellana

Bowl with horse breaker, from the Petrina necropolis at Narce, second half of the 7th cent. BC. Museo Nazionale Etrusco di Villa Giulia, Rome

Lebes on openwork foot, from the Pizzo Piede necropolis at Narce, first half of the 7th cent. BC. Museo Nazionale Etrusco di Villa Giulia, Rome

At the end of the 6th cent. BC the Faliscan territory saw the decline of some centers and the rise of others. For example Narce, located to the north, was eclipsed by Falerii (the modern Civita Castellana), which came to dominate the area. However, the presence of a protohistoric necropolis at nearby Montarano seems to indicate its antiquity, even though at that time the residential part of Falerii was located on the hill of Vignale, already occupied in the 8th and 7th centuries. Its growth at the beginning of the 5th century is documented by a complicated urban restructuring that gave prominence to the places of worship in the area of the settlement and its immediate surroundings. In addition to the temple on Vignale (5th cent. BC), the sacred complex of Lo Scasato was laid out in the zone to the east of the plateau. Brought to light in 1886-87, it comprised a large square basin, 13 m on a side and 8 deep, excavated in the rock and equipped with two flights of steps; the temple proper had a podium of blocks of tuff with a 17-m-wide front facing west. Numerous pieces of terracotta facing, such as *acroteria* with palmettes and slabs carved in relief, were found on the site, as well as fragments of statues from the pediment. These included a seated man, the torso of a youth and parts of draped women and men. Stylistic analysis suggests that a smaller *sacellum* had stood on the site earlier, in the late 4th-early 3rd cent. BC, but was demolished during the destruction of the city in 241 BC. In its place was built the new temple, whose terracottas date in fact from the second

Terracotta head of a man from the temple of Lo Scasato at Falerii, first half of the 4th cent. BC. Museo Nazionale Etrusco di Villa Giulia, Rome

Opposite, small terracotta head of Mercury, from the larger temple of Vignale at Falerii Veteres, first half of the 3rd cent. BC. Museo Nazionale Etrusco di Villa Giulia, Rome

half of the 3rd cent. BC, and were then restored in the 2nd-1st cent. BC. The votive material, which includes a model of a sheep's liver with instructions for divination (haruspicy), ceased to accumulate on its final destruction (mid-1st cent. BC).

Some of the finds from this temple are now on display in the Museo Archeologico dell'Agro Falisco at Civita Castellana, while the rest can be seen at the Museo di Villa Giulia in Rome, along with the ones from the suburban sanctuaries of Celle and the Sassi Caduti. The place of worship at Celle was dedicated to Juno Quirites and is mentioned by Dionysius of Halicarnassus, who described it as very like the one in Argos, with similar sacrificial rites, establishing a link with the Argive origin of the Falisci. The sanctuary of the Sassi Caduti, dating from the early 5th century, was decorated with acroterial figures of warriors and antefixes with satyrs carrying off maenads, the work of Etruscan craftsmen.

The connection between Falerii and the Etruscan world is clear not just from the

The walls of Falerii Novi and, below, detail of the Gate of Jupiter

archeological evidence but also from the literary sources, which tell us that the Faliscan city offered its support to Veii for the defense of Fidenae in 437 BC, and then sided with Tarquinii against Rome. The conflict with Rome was marked by a series of episodes prior to its submission in 293 BC, and then rebellion in 241, when the Romans massacred 15 000 Faliscans, destroyed the city and decided to rebuild it on a different site about 6 km away. The new center, appropriately called Falerii Novi, was ringed by walls stretching for over 2 km and lined with fifty square towers, to defend the city and its most important buildings. Some of these, like the amphitheater in the commune of Fabrica di Roma, are still visible today.

Sutri and Nepi

Sutri, located on a spur of tuff isolated by the courses of the Promonte and Rotoli rivers, stood at the center of an area occupied since prehistoric times and during the Early Iron Age. Chamber tombs dating from the 6th cent. BC have been identified, while much less is known of the city itself, apart from traces of the defensive walls in blocks of tuff, perhaps built the following century. The center served as a point of control over the corridor between the Cimini Mountains to the north and the Sabatini Mountains to the south, with their impenetrable forests, and provided the coastal cities, especially Caere, with a commercial outlet close to the Faliscan area, as well as a junction on the road from Nepi to Veii. It was after the fall of Veii in 396 BC that Sutri entered the Roman orbit, becoming a center of strategic control at the expense of the Falisci and the territories of Tarquinii. There were repeated and bloody conflicts with the latter until 311 BC, when Rome finally defeated Tarquinii and annexed Sutri.

The depopulation of the area caused by the constant warfare was compensated by the foundation of a colony of Campanians in 210 BC, who were offered land that included cleared areas of the Cimina and Sabatina forests. The opening of the Via Cassia and the creation of

View of the amphitheater at Sutri

Entrance of hypogeum carved out of the tuff in the archeological area of Sutri

The church of Santa Maria del Parto at Sutri, originally a rock Mithraeum

Front of the rock necropolis at Sutri

another colony (Colonia Coniuncta Iulia Sutrina) after the civil wars of the 1st cent. BC made it one of the most flourishing centers. This is evident from the remains we see today, all from the Roman era, such as the sections of the walls on the southwest and northeast sides, the rock Mithraeum converted into the church of the Madonna del Parto in the Middle Ages, a small complex of baths near the ancient forum and the amphitheater excavated in the living tuff, capable of holding 3-4000 spectators. From pre-Roman Sutri remain the Etruscan rock tombs, whose contents are in the local Museo del Patrimonium.

Nearby Nepi (Nepet to the Etruscans), whose cemeteries stretch back to the 7th cent. BC, was an important center of trade in the Archaic era, something that is reflected in the Attic pottery found in graves and in the roads that linked it to Sutri and Veii by what was to become the Via Amerina. Allied with Veii at the time of its fall, Nepi was caught up in the changing political fortunes of the area, disputed between Etruria and Rome. It was eventually absorbed by the Romans who founded a new colony for its control (383 or 373 BC). The economy of Nepi, like that of Sutri, went through a dark period, attested by the fact that the city was punished for refusing to pay tribute to Rome for the Hannibalic War (209 BC). Only with the opening of the Cassia did the settlement, like the rest of the area, regain a relative prosperity.

Veii (Veio)

Closely linked to the Faliscan area, Veii (Veis to the Etruscans, Veio in modern Italian) stood on the right bank of the Tiber above a vast plateau lapped by the Cremera (now Valchetta) and Piordo rivers. The city's wealth was based essentially on control of the Southern Valtiberina, through several fortified settlements, and exploitation of the salt pans at the Tiber's mouth, although the proximity to Rome (just 17 km) led to continual conflict, dating all the way back to the time of Romulus.

The locality appears to have been frequented since the Bronze Age, but only in the Iron Age (9th cent. BC) was the plateau of Veii settled, with huts arranged in several groups that alternated with areas left free for the raising of sheep. The fusion of these communities gave rise to a city that soon covered an area of 190 hectares. Vast cemeteries, with well tombs in the oldest phase and pit tombs in the following period (8th cent. BC), lined the main roads that linked the settlement of Veii to

satellite centers in the area. In the Orientalizing period these gave way to pit burials with loculi to hold the grave goods and the chamber tomb made its appearance. One of these, at Riserva del Bagno (second quarter of 7th cent. BC), was painted with figures of ducks. Another rare tomb found in the necropolis of Monte Michele (called the Campana Tomb after its discoverer) and painted with figures of real and imaginary animals and people riding horses that are now hard to decipher, dates from later still (end of 7th cent. BC). A "princely" tomb has recently been excavated at the same locality, and its rich contents, along with other evidence, like the burial mounds at Vacchereccia and Monte Aguzzo, where the celebrated *Chigi Olpe* of Corinthian manufacture (Museo di Villa Giulia) was found, bear witness to the remarkable flourishing of the city in the Orientalizing period.

During the 6th century Veii was given a truly urban layout. Walls were built out of blocks of tuff, along with numerous sanctuaries decorated with slabs produced in the fa-

The *Apollo* from the sanctuary of Portonaccio at Veio, late 6th cent. BC. Museo Nazionale Etrusco di Villa Giulia, Rome

Views of the remains of the sanctuary of Portonaccio

mous local workshops. At Campetti there was a temple dedicated to a goddess of the underworld with the same name as the city, Veis, the equivalent of the Latin Ceres, and near Piazza d'Armi stood the great sanctuary of Juno Regina, the city's guardian deity, which has now been excavated. But the best known of the sanctuaries lay outside the walls, on a site sheer above the Mola River at Portonaccio. Dedicated to Minerva and already in existence in the 7th cent. BC, the building went through various phases of construction and ornamentation, including the extraordinary one at the end of the 6th century, when it was adorned with beautiful clay statues of gods made by the local sculptor Vulca. Although some of these

were lost as the place went into decline, the surviving groups are now in the Museo di Villa Giulia.

In the 5th century the city's history was marked by clashes with Rome over the control of Fidenae, a settlement located in a strategic position on the left bank of the Tiber that allowed it to control trade with the Northern Valtiberina. It was in 479 BC, at the Cremera River, that the army of Veii crushed a Roman one made up of members of the family of the Fabii. Over the course of these struggles, King Larth Tulumnes lost his life during the second half of the century, defeated and killed by Cornelius Cossus. The spoils of the Etruscan monarch were dedicated to Jupiter at his tem-

Terracotta statuette of Aeneas carrying his father Anchises from the sacred area of Campetti at Veio, first half of the 5th cent. BC. Museo Nazionale Etrusco di Villa Giulia, Rome

Interior of the tomb of the Ducks, second quarter of the 7th cent. BC

Cinerary urn in the form of a Canopic jar with a human face on a throne, late 8th cent. BC; *olla* with painted boat, second half of the 8th cent. BC, from the necropolis of Olmo Bello at Bisenzio. Museo Nazionale Etrusco di Villa Giulia, Rome

ple in Rome, where the cuirass with a dedicatory inscription was still preserved in the time of Augustus. The capture of Fidenae and its destruction in 426 BC allowed the Romans to launch a decisive attack on Veii, allied solely with the Faliscan cities of Falerii and Capena but abandoned by the other peoples of the Etruscan League because of its monarchic rule. Long besieged by Rome, it fell after ten years of hard fighting to the dictator Furius Camillus, who brought the statue of Juno Regina back to Rome, where it was installed on the Aventine. This opened the way to the conquest of Southern Etruria.

From this moment Veii lost its importance, but was not abandoned. Indeed some of its sanctuaries were still capable of drawing large numbers of people. The one at Portonaccio was still in use up until the 2nd cent. BC, when the altar of Minerva was dismantled and destroyed. In the Augustan age the city became a *municipium*, occupying only a small part of the immense area that had been covered by the Etruscan city.

Bisenzio

The area around Lake Bolsena was also a crossroads of cultural exchange and communications. While the Western side of the lake came fully within the area of Vulci's influence, the territory to the north belonged to Volsinii, the powerful Etruscan city that has been identified with modern Orvieto. This zone was already extensively occupied in the Early Iron Age, as the Villanovan finds made at Orvieto as well as at Bolsena-Gran Carro and Bisenzio show. The remains of earlier settlements from the end of the Bronze Age have been identified at the latter locality too, on the summit of Monte Bisenzo, and it is likely that various small communities were also present on the level ground now covered by the waters of the lake.

The most significant testimonies to Bisenzio between the middle of the 8th century and the end of the next come from its cemeteries, located to the south of the mountain (at Piantana, Olmo Bello, Le Bucacce, La Polledrara, Porto Madonna and San Bernardino), as well as to its west (Poggio Sambuco, Valle Spinetto, Valle Saccoccia, Poggio della Mina and Palazzetta) and north (San Magno, Mereio and Poggio Falchetto). The finds made here are among the prize exhibits of the collections now on show at the Museo di Villa Giulia in Rome. The local culture whose aspects are reflected by the grave goods of the Villanovan phase is characterized by the rarity of biconical cinerary urns and the prevalence of hut urns instead, along with the richness of plastic decorations. While some pieces of particular significance are already known for the pre-Etruscan era, such as the hut urn from Olmo Bello, it was between the 8th and 7th cent. BC that the center displayed signs of a sudden in-

Bronze candelabrum with cockerel, late 6th cent. BC; cinerary urn in bronze plate with scene of ritual dance, late 8th cent. BC; incense-burner cart, second half of the 8th cent. BC, from the necropolis of Olmo Bello at Bisenzio. Museo Nazionale Etrusco di Villa Giulia, Rome

crease in prosperity, especially where bronze artifacts are concerned. Typical of the local production is the presence of small figures cast from solid bronze and applied as ornaments to cinerary urns, carts and amphorae, made out of embossed plate. While the prototypes for this method of decoration were Oriental products, the choice of the themes depicted and the predilection for crowded scenes in which spectacular effect and narrative content are preferred over refinement of detail appears totally autonomous and local in origin.

One of the most significant examples is the incense-burner cart, used in religious ceremonies, found in Tomb II at Olmo Bello and dated to the second half of the 8th century. The crosspieces linking the wheels to the support of the receptacle are thronged with figures of warriors, women carrying amphorae on their heads, a plowman with a pair of oxen and a hunter with an animal on a leash; in other words scenes of daily life and activities characteristic of members of society whose status was growing at the time.

Equally important is the amphora made of bronze plate (late 8th cent. BC) from Tomb XXII at Olmo Bello, whose shoulder and lid are decorated with two circular scenes, perhaps to be interpreted as moments in a religious ceremony connected with hunting or war. In fact it is possible to recognize various armed men, along with a man driving an ox, a figure that may be a prisoner with his hands tied and, at the center of the lid, what is probably a bear with a chain around its neck, apparently performing the function of a totem animal.

The richness of Bisenzio is testified by the jewelry and ornaments made of amber, for example the *bullae* and *fibulae* from Tomb II at Olmo Bello, as well as by the assimilation of figurative models of the late Geometric type, whose distinctive features show that they were introduced here through Vulci and Tarquinii. These two cities also exercised a political influence, but this waned over the course of the 7th cent. BC, a development that went hand in hand with a decadence in the style of the metal artifacts and pottery, which ended up repeating obsolete schemes. From the 6th century date a number of chamber tombs, located chiefly to the north of the built-up area, and tombs with chests of tuff, from which come black-figure vases, *bucchero* ware and bronzes, now in the Museo di Villa Giulia. While the objects found in the area date from as late as the end of the 5th century, it is clear that it had entered a profound crisis. The site was occupied again in the 3rd cent. BC with the establishment of a Roman *municipium* and the introduction of the Latin cult of Minerva Nortina.

The Area around Volsinii

Early Iron-Age crockery from the lake settlement of the Gran Carro on Bolsena Lake.
Museo Civico Rocca Monaldeschi, Bolsena

What is now the headland of Gran Carro, on Lake Bolsena, was originally just one segment of the territory occupied by a village in the Early Iron Age. Underwater investigations have identified the remains of numerous lake dwellings, whose piles have been preserved in the mire. In fact the level of the lake has risen over the centuries, and studies have shown that by the beginning of the Iron Age it was 4 m higher than in the preceding Bronze Age. In the 7th-6th cent. BC the level grew by another 5 m, and since then two more have been added. Taken altogether, the underwater finds in this lake of volcanic origin, already numerous for the middle of the II millennium BC, have made it possible to measure the increase in the water level with precision. Among the various discoveries from the Villanovan era, that of the Gran Carro is the most significant. The settlement was originally protected to the east by a rocky overhang and to the north by an elevation, as well as by a large dry-stone structure in the form of a truncated cone that was more than 3 m high and had an elliptical base measuring over 50 x 70 m, on which an open space of around 35 x 55 m was laid out. Erected on a site where hot water and gas come to the surface, the structure may date back as far as the Bronze Age, given the presence of potsherds from this period, and have had a defensive function. Hundreds of piles of about 20-30 cm in diameter have been identified in its vicinity, relating to a lake settlement of the Early Iron Age covering an area of more than 6000 sq. m. The dwellings were rectangular, and perhaps arranged in parallel strips set about 3 m apart. A road, of which some traces emerge from the water, linked the village to other settlements on the lakeshore. Along with spindle whorls, mallets, chisels, *fibulae* and bits, the finds have included biconical vases for water or foodstuffs, cup-pails with tall handles, jars, jugs, mugs, bowls and *impasto* cooking stoves in the form of a truncated cone. A distinctive feature is the presence of rounded vases with spouts communicating with the interior, perhaps used as oil lamps with several wicks. A short distance away, a 10-m long dugout made from a single tree trunk has been identified on the lake bed. The abandonment of the place seems to have been connected with the rise of the lake, which as has already been suggested forced the population to look for new sites.

Volsinii (Orvieto)

View of Orvieto

The "Venus," sculpture in Greek marble from the sanctuary of the Cannicella Necropolis, 530-520 BC. Museo Claudio Faina, Orvieto

Volsinii, or Velzna in Etruscan, from which modern Orvieto sprang, was located to the northeast of the lake and set on a steep tuff crag that rose about 40 m above the plain traversed by the Paglia River. To the Villanovan phase date some of the materials from the town (excavated near the place where the church of Sant'Andrea now stands), from sites then occupied by the necropolises of Cannicella and Crocifisso del Tufo and from several pit tombs. Not very numerous, these finds of pottery and metal ware do not suggest that the oldest settlement was particularly prosperous. Over the course of the 7th cent. BC, however, there are clear signs of growth, to be attributed not just to the agricultural potential of the area, but also to the settlement's strategic position at the confluence of the Paglia and Tiber. Both rivers were navigable and, connected in turn with other watercourses, provided easy means of communication between Volsinii and the Clusium area and the territories of Vulci and the Falisci.

The oldest part of the necropolis of the Cannicella, located on the southern side, where the chamber tombs with pitched roofs are set on terraces, dates from the Orientalizing phase of Volsinii. Their contents include fine *bucchero* ware, examples of a local production that has been widely studied and is characterized by a sober decoration enriched with bands of figures, made by rolling cylinders with the design cut into them over the clay while still soft.

Unusually, the lowest part of the cemetery, housed a sanctuary from the last quarter of the 6th century devoted to funerary and fertility cults, bounded by a sturdy retaining wall and composed of various structures. To the south it had an open area of paving with channels connected to a central basin for purifying ablutions, flanked by a similar space with a basin and well. Adjoining this was the only covered space, as the architectural terracottas found on the site demonstrate, which had a sunken jar, perhaps used for purifications, and a channel at the center. The materials unearthed there included the famous statue of Greek marble known as the *Cannicella Venus*, now on display at the Museo Faina along with other masterpieces from Volsinii. It represents a nude woman and may have been sculpted on Naxos, judging by the material employed, between 530 and 520 BC. The figure, whose calf and breast were restored in antiquity, was adapted to the needs of Etruscan forms of worship by the carving of holes to hold characterizing objects. Used to venerate the goddess of fertility, it must have been identified with Mater Matuta, an Etruscan deity known to us only from Latin literary sources, or, going by some of the inscriptions, Veis. The sanctuary was further enlarged over the course of the 4th century, allowing the nearby necropolis to maintain its importance in a period in which the other cemeteries in the area went into decline.

Two views of the necropolis of Crocefisso del Tufo

The other large burial ground, to the northwest of the city, is the necropolis of Crocefisso del Tufo, laid out during the 6th century according to a systematic plan of an urbanistic type. It contains a range of modular tombs, arranged in a grid with blocks separated by streets that intersect at right angles. Each individual chamber tomb, essentially identical to the others, was built out of ashlars of tufaceous stone that formed two walls, an outer and an inner, with the gap between them filled with earth and pebbles. A doorway with a lintel led into a vestibule that gave in turn onto the rectangular cell, covered with a corbel vault that turned it into a sort of small, pointed nave. A platform running along the rear

The foundations of the Belvedere Temple, 5th cent. BC

Terracotta Heracles from the Belvedere Temple, late 5th-early 4th cent. BC. Museo Archeologico Nazionale, Orvieto

wall and one side wall was used to deposit the corpses and grave goods.

The assignment of the tombs to families (mostly from the middle classes), with the deceased's name placed above the door, was evidently carried out by public bodies, whose ability to plan and manage works on such a scale bears witness to the stability of the Volsinian community in the Archaic era. Study of the epigraphs and the characteristics of the names has revealed that the tombs were registered to women too, and that ancient Volsinii was inhabited not just by Etruscans, but also by people of Italic and Celtic origin. The contents of the tombs at Crocefisso del Tufo, which include imported Attic pottery, attest to the affluence of the local families in the 6th and 5th century, and to the high artistic level attained by the local potters and metal workers.

The urban area in antiquity appears to have coincided with that of modern Orvieto, and while this fact has made excavation difficult, it has at least preserved the access from the southwest, now Porta Maggiore. No residential districts have come to light, but numerous places of worship have been found in various parts of the city, of which the best-known and most legible is the temple of the Belvedere. Identified in the 19th century, it was built at the rear of a square sacred precinct, whose boundary walls joined up with the front of the temple. It stood on a podium that was partly cut out of the living rock and partly constructed, with a ramp or flight of steps providing access. The pronaos in front, with one side at a slight angle, had two rows of four columns with a diameter of 1 m that preceded the three cells. Overall, the plan has exactly the same proportions as the architect Vitruvius stated were those of the Tuscan style of temple, typical of the Etruscans, in his *De Architectura*. The oldest facing materials of the building date from the beginning of the 5th cent. BC, while the majority of the pedimental sculptures are from the 5th-6th century and come from the pediment at the rear. Their high

Two antefixes from the Belvedere Temple, late 5th-early 4th cent. BC. Museo Archeologico Nazionale, Orvieto

Wall with biga in the tomb of the Hescanas, near Porano, late 4th-early 3rd cent. BC

quality, profoundly influenced by the style of Phidias, has led historians to suggest that Greek artists were present in Volsinii. In addition to the remains of *acroteria* (with sphinxes and gorgons) and antefixes, a few fragments of the front pediment with warriors have been found. Among the votive offerings are a number of dedicatory inscriptions, one of which indicates Tinia Calusna, i.e. Jupiter the hurler of thunderbolts, as the deity worshiped here.

Various groups of architectural terracottas connected with places of worship, or with sculptors' workshops, have been brought to light in the urban area. However, it has not been possible to identify the temple of the goddess Nortia to which Livy referred when he described the tradition of driving a nail into the wall of this temple in Volsinii every year to mark the passing of time, in a similar way to what was prescribed by an ancient law at the temple of Jupiter Optimus Maximus in Rome.

Even better known in the literary tradition was the sanctuary called Fanum Voltumnae, dedicated to Voltumna, an Archaic Etruscan deity who personified the principle of transformation and change in nature and life. The sanctuary outside the city walls was used to stage festivities and periodic spectacles that were attended by representatives of the "Twelve Peoples" of Etruria, i.e. the most powerful urban communities, in an attempt to establish a political cooperation similar to what had been achieved in Greece through the leagues of cities. Never identified with certainty, this sanctuary may have stood in the area of Campo della Fiera, where a place of worship with artifacts and structures has been brought to light.

At the time of the first conflicts with Rome, Volsinii seems to have seen a shift in the focus of its economic activities, hitherto characterized by the production of painted ware and silver-plated pottery, toward the farming of the territory, documented by a reduction in the number of burials in some urban cemeteries

and the presence of various settlements in the surrounding countryside. Among the chamber tombs found at Poggio di Molinella, that of the Hescanas family, decorated between the 4th and 3rd cent. BC with polychrome paintings of scenes of the afterlife and destined to remain in use for a long time, can still be visited. Other groups of graves were present in the territory, for instance at Settecamini, where chamber tombs were excavated in the tuff, including the two well-known Golini Tombs. The first (Golini I), preceded by a sloping passageway that led down to the quadrangular chamber with a short central screen, dates from the middle of the 4th cent. BC. It was adorned with paintings of high quality, now on display

at the Museo Archeologico in Orvieto, representing the preparations for a banquet. The client was portrayed to the right of the entrance, arriving in the other world on a two-horse chariot escorted by a winged demon. Slightly more recent (second half of the 4th century), Golini Tomb II also had a single chamber and was decorated with paintings of the hereafter. The nearby tomb of the Warrior was roughly contemporary, and its rich contents included a dinner service (two *situlae*, a jug and a low decorated cup) accompanied by a complete set of bronze armor.

While the neighboring rural centers prospered and the city's area of influence was expanded, perhaps as far as the Clusium region

Detail of the wall decoration of the Golini I Tomb, second half of the 4th cent. BC. Museo Archeologico Nazionale, Orvieto

(as is demonstrated by the characteristics of the painted tomb recently discovered at Sarteano), Volsinii, owing to its domination of the lines of communication, found itself caught up in a struggle with Rome. Clashes took place between the two cities in 392, in 308 (with the defeat at Lake Vadimone) and again in 294, 285 and 280 BC. According to the literary sources, this state of conflict, together with the growth in the lower class, some of whom came from non-Etruscan ethnic groups, produced a difficult internal political situation. The social pressure from the serfs (something for which there is also archeological evidence in the form of the presence of the names of cooks in the frescoes of the Golini Tombs) and the discontent of the lower classes became uncontainable. After repeated uprisings, the city's rulers were forced to grant the slaves their freedom, as well as the right to hold public posts. However, this threat to the predominance of the ancient nobility induced the aristocracy to make secret contacts with the Romans, who were asked to intervene directly. This resulted in the expedition led by Fulvius Flaccus, which conquered and destroyed the city in 264 BC. The population or, as they are described in the literary sources "the natives of Volsinii and the serfs who had remained loyal to their masters," were moved from their original homes to a less protected site, in the vicinity of the lake: Bolsena, given the name of Volsinii Novi.

Bolsena

Remains of buildings from the Etrusco-Roman period

Archeological investigations have shown that Bolsena was not occupied until the 3rd cent. BC. Among its oldest structures are the walls in *opus quadratum*, which stretched for almost 4.5 km. Letters in the Etruscan alphabet can still be seen on the ramparts of the castle. Also ascribable to that initial period in the city's history are several chamber tombs at Poggio Pesce and the suburban sanctuaries of the

Pozzarello and Poggio Casetta, both of them open to the public. Dated erroneously to the Archaic era, the small temple with a single rectangular room at Poggio Casetta actually has features typical of the urban and suburban shrines of the 6th and 5th cent. BC, akin, for example, to the ones at Fiesole. Its archaizing appearance has been attributed by some to the modest standard of living at Volsinii Novi in

the first few decades of its existence, as well as to an ideological nostalgia for a past with which the forced move had created a sharp break. After around a century of adjustment under what were not initially flourishing economic circumstances (the city was unable of contribute aid to Rome during the Second Punic War), Bolsena was given a strong boost in the 2nd cent. BC with the opening of the Via Cassia, which passed through the city. This resulted in a substantial modification in the urban layout, which was divided up again into blocks by new *cardines* and *decumani*, although the more hilly areas maintained a high density of population, as the atrium houses of Poggio Moscini datable to just this phase demonstrate. The numerous workshops in the archeological area were constructed in the republican period, while the aqueduct, the baths with their *cryptoporticus* (*calidarium* and cistern) and the paved forum that provided access to the basilica date from the 1st cent. AD. The remains of these buildings, destroyed on the abandonment of the city in the 6th century at the time of the Visigoth and Longobard invasions, are currently open to the public. (M.M.)

Clay throne with panthers from Bolsena, 2nd cent. BC. Museo Civico Rocca Monaldeschi, Bolsena

Remains of walls with engraved Etruscan letters

Places of Worship

Over the span of Etruscan civilization buildings constructed for the purposes of worship underwent a constant evolution, linked not just to technical and structural factors but also to religious and symbolic ones, turning them in the course of time into something more than mere "containers" for effigies and sacred rites: they became a sort of emblem of the higher heavenly order.

In the early Iron Age worship was practiced both in the open air and in specially built huts or shelters, which were also used to hold religious feasts and, perhaps, to house the common assets of the village. The Latin term, *templum*, was used among other things for the hut of the augurs who observed the sky for divine omens.

With the Orientalizing period the *principes* who ruled communities,

Model of Etruscan temple from the votive deposit of the North Gate of Vulci, mid-1st cent. BC. Museo Nazionale Etrusco di Villa Giulia, Rome

Antefix with figure of Maenad from the temple of the Sassi Caduti at Falerii, early 5th cent. BC. Museo Nazionale Etrusco di Villa Giulia, Rome

invested with religious authority, moved the place of worship into a space inside their palaces. An echo of this may be found in the *temenos*, the square sacred area that would be a constant feature of later Etruscan sanctuaries.

The crisis in the monarchic system that began to emerge around the 6th century resulted in a separation of religion from political power and its subsequent administration by priests, who used a new, public location: the temple. Usually paid for by voluntary contributions from aristocrats – if not erected as a votive offering – its forms were influenced by the appearance of earlier sacred structures, based on established principles and consolidated rituals.

The places of worship with the simplest plan were rectangular buildings in the form of an aedicule with a single enclosed space, or with two columns on the front, as can be seen in a number of votive models. Around these shrines, generally at the front and the sides, ran an enclosure designed to prevent those who had not purified themselves from seeing or taking part in the rituals. Such areas, bounded in the simplest cases with fences or curtains – also called *templa* in Latin – were in others more permanently screened by a wall (*temenos*), as at the shrine of Poggio Casetta in Bolsena, although this is of fairly late date, or those of archaic Fiesole.

However, the typical archaic and classical temple (called *tmia* in Etruscan, judging by the plaques found at Pyrgi) was of much larger

proportions and had a colonnaded portico – a *pronaos*, to use the Greek term – that occupied the front half. In the rear part there were three small, adjoining *naoi* or, more frequently, a central room (*cella*) flanked by two narrow rooms, open at the front (*alae*). In his *De Architectura* (IV, 7), the Roman architect Vitruvius has left us a detailed although late (last quarter of 1st cent. BC) description of this building and its structure. Archeological discoveries, such as the temple of the Belvedere in Orvieto, have proved the truth of his claim that the preferred ratio between front and side was five to six.

The side walls of the Etruscan temple sometimes extended all the way to the front, to form *antae* enclosing the columns (always in rows of an even number), which in such cases were called *in antis*, i.e. "between the *antae*," as in the Hellenistic temple at Fiesole. Above the colonnade at the front ran a wooden architrave covered with decorated and painted slabs of terracotta. From this projected longitudinal beams (*mutuli* in Latin) faced with decorated clay panels at the end. Other panels, as in temple A at Pyrgi, protected the ends of the crossbeam of the roof (*columen*), on which rested the *cantherii* that formed the two pitches. In the oldest buildings the triangle formed in this way was closed by wooden planks; a small sloping surface inside at the front helped to drain rainwater. It was only in a later period that triangular pediments were introduced, on the

Acroterion from the temple of the Sassi Caduti at Falerii, early 5th cent. BC. Museo Nazionale Etrusco di Villa Giulia, Rome

Greek model, decorated with complex groups of terracotta sculptures like those on the famous pediment at Talamone. Previously a few statues had occasionally been located on the crossbeam, as in the temple of the Portonaccio at Veio. In general, however, brightly colored terracotta decorations covered the wooden parts of the roof, to protect them from the weather and from parasites; special terminal tiles with heads or figures – called antefixes – were set along the edges of the roof.

In the vicinity of the temple there were often a pool of water for sacred ablutions and curative immersions, one or more altars and several buildings for use as a hostel. Over time, in fact, it became common for large numbers of pilgrims to visit the sanctuaries, leading to the creation of fairs and markets near the best-known places of worship. The worshippers included people from Magna Graecia and Carthage, whose visits were encouraged by special cults with the aim of developing good diplomatic and commercial relations. Various hypotheses have been put forward on the origin of the architectural module of the Etruscan temple, all of which may contain a part of the truth. Many elements of the oldest huts of the Iron Age were undoubtedly preserved, although transformed: the peculiar canopy located inside the triangle of the pediment was nothing but a

"monumentalized" form of the covering set above the hole made in the roof of the hut to let out smoke. The marked frontality of the building and the presence of columns only at the front are features derived from the hut of straw and mud, just as the statues and the ornamental volutes of the sanctuaries are echoes of its carved beams.

As far as the plan is concerned, it is believed by some that the large temples were derived from the smaller shrines that have already been described, with the small room used for worship becoming the inner *cella* and the *temenos* as a whole transformed into the temple proper and its open portico. Another hypothesis suggests that the

proportions of the shrines with a single room were expanded to contain a small *cella* set against the rear wall, a sort of *sancta sanctorum* used to house the idol for worship. According to a possible reconstruction based on what survives, the temple in Piazza d'Armi at Veio provides evidence in support of this hypothesis, although there is some uncertainty over the actual plan of the building. However, the coexistence of small shrines and proper temples in the period following the 6th cent. BC indicates that the different types of building must also have been connected with different practices of worship, as is claimed in the Latin literary sources. (M.M.)

Bottom left, antefix from the sanctuary of the Cannicella Necropolis, late 6th-early 5th cent. BC. Museo Archeologico Nazionale, Orvieto; center and right, antefixes from the sanctuary of Portonaccio at Veio, late 6th cent. BC. Museo Nazionale Etrusco di Villa Giulia, Rome

The Museo Archeologico Nazionale in Orvieto

Housed in the picturesque setting of Martin IV's palace, the Archeological Museum contains the materials formerly in the collection of the Cathedral Vestry Board, along with finds made in more recent excavations carried out in several sanctuaries in the city and in the surrounding burial grounds. Arranged in topographical and partly chronological order, it represents a sort of complement to the Museo Faina, so that the two institutions offer a fairly complete picture of the ancient Etruscan settlement of Orvieto. Particularly interesting are the numerous grave goods uncovered in the nearby necropolises of Crocifisso del Tufo and Cannicella, as well as the materials excavated in recent times at Castellonchio, which include a large quantity of bronzes and jewelry from the Hellenistic era.

Also on display in the museum are the paintings from the Golini I and Golini II Tombs (named after the man who found them), detached for reasons of conservation and remounted in the museum in a reconstruction of their original subterranean location. The two graves, dated to the second half of the 4th cent. BC, were brought to light in 1863 at the locality of Settecamini near Porano, one of the villages in the vicinity of the crag.

The Golini I Tomb, quadrangular in plan and divided into two chambers by a screen, had walls covered with plaster on which the pictures had been painted. The frescoes depict a feast in honor of the deceased in the presence of the

gods of the underworlds Hades and Persephone, as we are told by the inscriptions set alongside each of the figures. They show the larder of the Etruscan family, stocked with various butchered animals hanging from hooks and ready for cooking. A large group of servants is engaged in the preparation of food, to the accompaniment of music performed by an accurately represented double-flute player. The Golini II Tomb, in an extremely precarious state of

preservation, also presents an image of a banquet accompanied by a procession of flautists and horn and cithara players, while the journey of the deceased to the afterworld is depicted on the entrance wall.

The room opposite the reconstruction of the two tombs houses numerous materials discovered in the necropolises of Settecamini, including bronze objects and Etruscan red-figure pottery of the 4th cent. BC. From the same period

One of the rooms on the ground floor

Reconstruction of the Golini I Tomb at Settecamini

The complete set of armor from the tomb of the Warrior at Settecamini, second half of the 4th cent. BC

Kylix with erotic scene from tomb 26 of the necropolis of Crocefisso del Tufo

Rhyton representing the face of Silenus from tomb 37 of the Fondo Bracardi at Orvieto

Mirror with winged figure from the necropolis of Porano

Kernos with women's faces from the necropolis of Settecamini

comes the beautiful bronze armor found in the Tomb of the Warrior, complete with helmet, anatomical cuirass, greaves (used to protect the legs) and shield.

There is a substantial collection of architectural terracottas which adorned the many sanctuaries in Etruscan Orvieto, among them the remains of the decorative pediment of the Belvedere Temple, datable to between the end of the 5th and the early 4th century. Of similar age is the beautifully crafted clay head of Tinia-Zeus from the sacred building on Via San Leonardo, while the remains of the decoration of the sanctuary of Cannicella are older (beginning of the 5th cent. BC). They include a central acroterion of considerable interest, interpreted as a representation of the sacrifice of Polyxena. (G.P.)

The Museo Archeologico "Claudio Faina"

In 1954 Count Claudio Faina donated his archeological collection to the city of Orvieto along with the building that housed it, located in front of the cathedral, where it had been transferred almost a century earlier from the family residence near Perugia. The contents of the museum, which constitute a collection of national significance, are subdivided into categories of object and housed on two stories of the building. Some parts have been fitted with period furniture in order to recreate the 19th-century antiquarian milieu that led to the

formation of the collection (1864), in particular the study of Count Mauro who put together the rich numismatic section.

The original core of the collection consisted of a group of vases sold to the Faina family by Princess Valentini Bonaparte, daughter of Lucien Bonaparte, the fortunate discoverer of the necropolises at Vulci. Initially enlarged with materials of various origins acquired on the antique market, the collection was further enriched by Count Eugenio with the finds made in excavations carried out

Amphora attributed to the Berlin Painter representing Heracles and the sea monster, from the necropolis of Crocefisso del Tufo, second half of the 6th cent. BC

Detail of the amphora attributed to the Chiusi Painter representing Achilles and Ajax playing dice, from the necropolis of Crocefisso del Tufo, second half of the 6th cent. BC

Amphora with panther, first quarter of the 6th cent. BC

Amphorae from the "Vanth group," late 4th cent. BC

in the local necropolises of Crocifisso del Tufo and Cannicella.

Particular importance in the layout of the museum is assigned to Attic black-figure pottery (represented by three large *amphorae* by Exekias, one of the greatest vase painters of the second half of the 6th cent. BC), red-figure pottery and the collection of Etruscan figurative ceramics. Among the latter it is worth singling out the vessels belonging to the so-called "Vanth group", after the name of the Etruscan divinity who accompanied the deceased into the underworld and who is portrayed on two pots in the museum, as well as the vases decorated by the Micali Painter.

The collection of *bucchero* ware

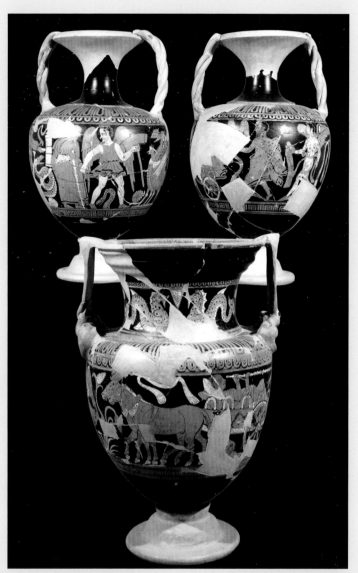

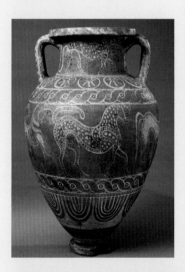

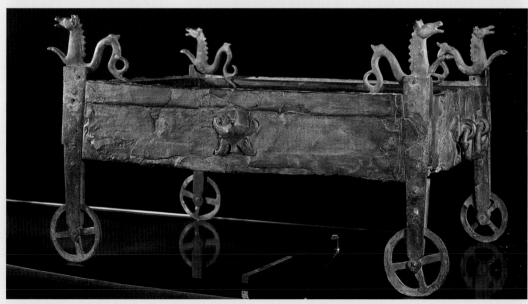

Bronze *foculus* with seahorses, early 5th cent. BC

Head of sarcophagus representing Ulysses and Circe from Torre San Severo, late 4th cent. BC

Gorgon from the Belvedere Temple, late 5th cent. BC

Head of warrior in nenfro from the necropolis of Crocefisso del Tufo, 525 BC

three thousand in all, which constituted the main interest of the Faina family.

The municipal collection is housed in three rooms on the ground floor of the building, annexed to the museum. It includes a group of ornamental terracottas, excavated near the sanctuary of the Belvedere and the sacred area of Via San Leonardo, the so-called "Cannicella Venus", a statue of a naked goddess made by a workshop in the east of Greece, and a monumental late 4th-cent. BC sarcophagus from Torre San Severo. On the long sides – where traces of the original polychromy can still be seen – are represented the sacrifice of Trojan prisoners in honor of Patroclus and the sacrifice of Polyxena on Achilles' tomb, while on the short sides Ulysses appears twice, accompanied by the seer Tiresias and the sorceress Circe respectively. (G.P.)

comprises an extensive range of products of potteries in Chiusi and Orvieto, and the fine collection of bronzes, many of which still bear the marks of clumsy restorations carried out in the 19th century, come from workshops in the same areas.
The visit to the museum concludes with the large collection of coins, over

Opposite, terracotta head of old man from the Belvedere Temple, late 5th cent. BC

Hellenistic sarcophagus with reclining male figure

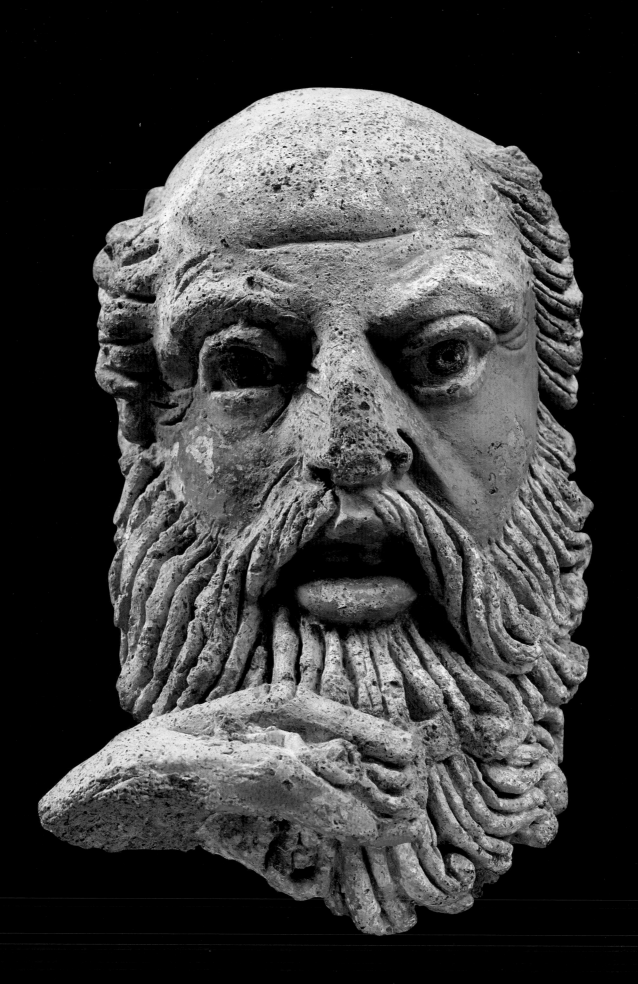

RUPESTRIAN ETRURIA

In a vast region to the south of Lake Bolsena whose landscape, still characterized by the dark green of the dense Mediterranean maquis, cannot be very different from the one inhabited by the ancient Etruscans, it is still possible to see superb expressions of that civilization, carved in stone. Entire "cities of the dead" sculpted out of the tuff and set in deep and picturesque gorges.

View of the rock necropolis of Castel d'Asso

Opposite, view of Tuscania with several sarcophagus lids on display in Piazza Basile

Structures of the Etruscan settlement

San Giovenale

Perhaps to be identified with the fortified settlement of Contenebra, mentioned by Livy as part of the territory of Tarquinii conquered by the Romans (389 BC), the Etruscan town at San Giovenale stood on a plateau of considerable strategic significance for the control of the upper valley of the Mignone. The remains of a small Bronze Age village with oval huts have been uncovered a short distance from the ruins of the 13th-century castle. This must have given way to a settlement made up of larger huts in the Iron Age, and then to the Etruscan one in the 7th century. A few of the dwellings from the latter have been found: quadrangular in plan, they consisted of two rooms with foundations constructed of blocks of tuff and walls of unfired brick. Houses of a similar kind have been excavated in an area to the east of the medieval castle. Sections of the walls that were built to defend the upper part of the town in the 4th century have also been brought to light.

The cemeteries are laid out around the hill of San Giovenale and contain well, box and tumulus tombs, as well as those cut from rock. The materials found in them suggest a cultural dependence on Caere in the oldest phase, and subsequently on Tarquinii.

Blera

Burial mound and, right, half-cube tombs

The ancient town cited by Pliny, Strabo and Ptolemy occupied part of a narrow shelf of tuff naturally defended by steep and high walls. Only a few remains of the settlement have come to light, chiefly sections of its massive walls, while those of the large necropolises that extended along the valleys of the Ricanale and Biedano are much more substantial. There is an evocative group of rock-cut tombs on the slope of Pian del Vescovo.

Several burial mounds derived from the cultural influence of Caere can be dated to the oldest phase (7th cent. BC), but it is the numerous cube and half-cube tombs of the 6th-5th cent. BC that are the most impressive sight. They have sculpted façades that in some cases show the structure of the pitched roof and the door leading to the mortuary chambers. The latter have platforms set against the walls or funeral beds with legs shaped like those of a *kline*. At the locality of Pian Gagliardo a tomb has been excavated with the vestiges of a painted decoration of simple ornamental motifs in a large mortuary chamber with a central column.

To the northwest and southeast of the modern town of Blera can still be seen the remains of two ancient bridges, the Ponte del Diavolo (with three arches) and Ponte della Rocca (with one arch), built in *opus quadratum* between the end of the 2nd cent. BC and the beginning of the 1st. Both structures were part of the consular Via Clodia, perhaps constructed at the turn of the 3rd cent. BC to link Saturnia with Rome through Western Etruria and using some stretches of earlier roads from the Etruscan period. In the Roman era Blera was a *municipium* assigned to the tribe Arnense.

Norchia

The Etruscan center was located in the middle section of a road that linked Blera with Tuscania, along a route subsequently followed by the consular Via Clodia. On the northern side of the ancient settlement, beyond a gate from the medieval era and the remains of a bridge with three arches over the Biedano River, almost 0.5 km of this evocative route (Cava Buia) is still visible, enclosed by sheer walls that reach a height of over 10 m. They bear Roman and medieval inscriptions, one of

Tombs with tympana in the rock necropolis of the 4th-3rd cent. BC

A view of the rock necropolis

Part of a tympanum carved with scenes of warriors, from the Hellenistic era necropolis of Norchia. Museo Archeologico, Florence

which may refer to repairs made to the road during the 1st cent. BC. The settlement at Norchia was also located on the important link between Tarquinii and Volsinii, which allowed it to exercise a function of control on behalf of the important coastal city. Modest vestiges of the ancient town survive, consisting largely of underground passages beneath the area occupied by the 13th-century castle and a few stretches of the ring of walls. The vitality of the settlement, most evident from the 4th century onward, is documented by a flourishing workshop of sculptors specializing in the production of sarcophagi. These were used not just for the burial of members of the local aristocracy,

but also sold to wealthy clients from the towns at Tuscania and San Giuliano.

The monumental tombs situated on the sides of the valleys of the Biedano, Acqualta and Pile, laid out in large cemeteries around the Etruscan town, are of great architectural interest. The tombs are lined up in two or three tiers along the valley walls and some of them housed members of eminent local families like the Churcle or Smurinas. Particularly fascinating are the tomb of the Three Heads, named after the sculptures that adorn the lintel of the mock door, and the Lattanzi Tomb, belonging to the Churcle family. Unfortunately in a poor state of preservation and partly overgrown with bushes, the tomb bears traces of a decoration with fantastic animals and floral elements. The two tombs with their fronts set side by side in the valley of the Acqualta have a monumental appearance. In imitation of contemporary sanctuaries, they have a colonnade supporting an architrave with a Doric frieze, surmounted by a pediment carved with mythological scenes and Gorgon's heads at the corners.

Castel d'Asso

On the basis of a famous oration by Cicero, the settlement at Castel d'Asso has been identified with the Roman Axia, one of the strongholds of the territory of Tarquinii. Very few archeological vestiges survive of the Etruscan town, which was set on a steep-sided plateau carved out by the Freddano and Risecco rivers. They consist chiefly of underground passages and shafts, along with fragments of decorative slabs from the Archaic period depicting Heracles and the Cretan bull which have been connected with a place of worship. Like other places in this region, Axia entered a period of considerable affluence in the 4th century, linked to its advantageous position on roads leading inland from the coast. From this time date the tombs with sumptuous architectural façades lining the valley of the Freddano, which have been classified into two different types: mock cube tombs (4th-3rd cent. BC) and tombs with a smaller façade under the main one (3rd-2nd cent. BC). The former have a mock door of the Doric type on the front, the others a lower section with a pitched roof (clearly in imitation of the houses of the living), that only in one case has a portico sup-

ported by columns. Some of the graves have deeply cut inscriptions on the front with the names of the deceased or numerals. Particularly interesting are the one known simply as the Large Tomb, which has a broad front with three doors, and the Orioli Tomb with a huge mortuary chamber intended to hold up to seventy burials.

Tuscania

Ensured a strategic role from time immemorial by its position at a crossroads, Tuscania also owed its prosperity to its location on a hill at the confluence of the Maschiolo and Marta rivers. One important road linked it with Tarquinii, another with Lake Bolsena and from there with inland Etruria and the valley of the Tiber. Easy communications were also possible with Norchia, Statonia, Musarna and Vulci, and the construction of the Via Clodia contributed to a great flowering of Tuscania between the 3rd and 1st cent. BC.

The Etruscan town stood on the hill (already inhabited in protohistoric times) now characterized by the imposing medieval complex of San Pietro, as is apparent from the re-

Oinochoe from Tuscania, late 4th cent. BC. Museo Archeologico Nazionale, Tuscania

Two nenfro sarcophagi made in Tuscania with reclining figures on their lids. Museo Archeologico Nazionale, Tuscania, and Museo Archeologico, Florence

mains of several walls in the area of the church and numerous underground passages linked to wells and cisterns. From the oldest phase of the settlement date several architectural decorations molded from clay (mid-6th cent. BC), similar in their iconography to examples from Acquarossa, as well as facing slabs with scenes of departure on a cart or with figures of horse riders clearly intended to glorify the ruling class of Tuscania.

The tombs of this period show that the town lay within the sphere of influence of Tarquinii, and this is confirmed by the contents of the graves. The monumental Cube Tomb in the necropolis of Peschiera is especially interesting as it provides an important clue to Etrus-

can residential architecture. Carved from a rib of rock, the tomb has a pitched roof, pediments on the short sides with mock beams and a central door. This leads into three rooms, two of them with carved beams on the ceiling. The large necropolises that are laid out around Tuscania (Peschiera, Pian di Mola, Ara del Tufo, Castelluzza) provide evidence for a major crisis during the 5th cent. BC and a notable cultural revival in the following century. The single-chamber tombs of the local aristocratic families (Vipinana, Statlane, Curunas) appear to have been in use for several generations, with the bodies interred in sarcophagi carved from nenfro, while the grave goods suggest close contacts with Tarquinii and the Faliscan area. Later on (3rd-2nd cent. BC) we find large tombs with platforms for many depositions and terracotta sarcophagi.

In the Roman era Tuscania was assigned to the Stellatina tribe, but maintained a thriving economy thanks to its strategic position, as is evident from the luxurious buildings decorated with mosaics that were constructed at the foot of the hill of San Pietro, imposing remains in *opus reticulatum*, stretches of paved road and ruins of baths: the so-called Bagni della Regina or "Queen's Baths."

Acquarossa

The ancient settlement at Acquarossa stood on a tufaceous plateau bounded by very deep valleys. Numerous buildings from the town that developed on this site between the 7th and 6th cent. BC have been excavated, providing precious information about the still little-known Etruscan architecture.

The dwellings, quadrangular in shape and with two or three rooms, occupied much of the plateau but were interspersed with areas for farming and grazing. Some of them had a vestibule at the front, or a portico set on wooden columns. The foundations were built of blocks of tufa and the walls of unfired brick, or constructed out of lattices, consisting of vertical poles that supported transverse frameworks of branches and reeds covered with clay. The complex wooden structure of the roof was made of beams covered with plain tiles and pantiles, sometimes embellished with lively

decorations that were repeated on slabs used to adorn the outside walls. For the survival of structures of this kind it was fundamental to control the flow of rainwater, which was collected and drained through channels. Special contrivances were also adopted to vent the smoke from the hearth, through a circular opening at the center of one of the tiles whose size could be adjusted by rotation of a disk. Some of the rooms in these houses were set

Antefix with a woman's face from zone F of Acquarossa, second half of the 6th cent. BC. Museo Civico, Viterbo

Decorative slabs representing a banquet (detail opposite) and Dionysian scene, from zone F of Acquarossa, second half of the 6th cent. BC. Museo Civico, Viterbo

aside for productive activities, such as weaving on a loom, or for the storage of foodstuffs.

In addition to public buildings and roads, a large structure identified as the residence of the aristocratic rulers of the town has been excavated in the archeological area. It was sumptuously decorated with slabs depicting two of Heracles' labors, the slaying of the Nemean lion and the capture of the bull on Crete, or banqueting scenes with reclining figures entertained by musicians. At the center of the building was set an open courtyard surrounded by a wooden colonnade, onto which opened a number of rooms that were only partly used as private dwellings. The settlement at Acquarossa, whose economy depended on farming and the raising of animals, was destroyed toward the end of the 6th cent. BC for reasons that are not yet entirely clear. From that moment on the site was abandoned. (G.P.)

Funerary Architecture

Unlike other civilizations that were contemporary with it, the Etruscan civilization did not resort to a single funerary rite but practiced cremation as well as interment throughout its existence. Whatever the reason may have been, it is a fact that the two rituals coexisted for centuries, suggesting an adherence to different religious formulas either on the basis of personal choice or because of the functions performed by the deceased in life, although bodies and ashes were often placed alongside one another in the great tombs of the nobility.

It is known, however, that cremation was the predominant funerary rite in the Villanovan period. After the body was burned on the pyre, the bones and ashes were placed in a vase covered by a bowl or helmet. This was then set at the bottom of a cylindrical shaft dug in the ground or carved in the living rock. Along with the vase, or cinerary urn, a number of objects that had belonged to the deceased were deposited in the tomb, such as spearheads, swords and cups for men or spindle whorls and crockery for women. The well was closed by a slab of stone that was sometimes convex on top, perhaps in

Below right, the entrance passage of the tomb of the Little Devil II at Vetulonia, last quarter of the 7th cent. BC

Detail of the corbel vault of the Montagnola Tomb, Quinto Fiorentino, late 7th cent. BC

Jar tomb containing a cinerary urn from the Guerruccia necropolis at Volterra, 8th cent. BC. Museo Etrusco Guarnacci, Volterra

imitation of a shield to provide magical protection; these slabs can be seen as the forerunners of the mounds of earth that were later erected over the large chamber tombs.

Contemporary with these well tombs were the pit tombs used for interment, which grew increasingly common as time passed: the body of the deceased was buried in a rectangular hole, together with a set of personal possessions.

The economic and social development of the 8th-7th cent. BC resulted in the organization of the population into large multifamily units, called *gentes*, who shared a common ancestor. This link was perpetuated even after death, at first by connecting the individual tombs of relatives with small channels and later by the custom of burying people belonging to the same *gens* in special areas reserved for them, which in the burial grounds of Vetulonia and Marsiliana took on the appearance of circles of stones. These circles housed the pits with the remains of the deceased, sometimes flanked by another quadrangular hole containing a large collection of weapons, dinner services and jewelry. The circle was probably topped by a mound of earth, no longer visible today as a consequence of the cultivation of the land.

The underground chamber tombs covered by tumuli or mounds evolved from the tombs described above. In fact the pit or well became too small and modest for the deposition of the rich grave goods of the Orientalizing period. Moreover the custom of creating "family chapels" made it necessary for the burial space to be easily reusable. The desire for a more marked monumentality on the outside went hand in hand, on the inside, with

the wish to make the house of the dead resemble that of the living. Sometimes effigies were even made of the deceased, as in the case of the Canopic jars of the Chiusi region, some statuettes from the area of Caere and rare traces of actual "dummies." Thus were born large tombs (7th and 6th cent. BC) contained in a low cylinder of stone, called a drum, over which a cone of the earth dug out was raised to protect the structures. An entrance and a downward sloping passage, known by the Greek term *dromos*, led to the underground chambers.

Depending on the type of stone found in the various parts of Etruria, some of these tombs were carved entirely from solid rock; in other cases they were partially or wholly constructed, like the Tomb of the Montagnola at Quinto Fiorentino, characterized by a particular method of realizing the roof that preceded the use of the vault. In the chamber tombs of the 6th cent. BC carved out of tuff, like the ones at Caere, the skill of the ancient artisans was sometimes able to reproduce the complicated plan of an aristocratic house, with several rooms laid out around a central *atrium*, complete with decorated doorways, seats and beds. Outside the sepulchers, open spaces for the temporary display of the body and the grave goods were occasionally created next to the mound: in all probability, periodical sacrifices on behalf of the deceased were

Interior of the tomb of the Reliefs in the Banditaccia necropolis at Cerveteri, second half of the 4th cent. BC

View of the rock necropolis of Sopraripa near Sovana

also carried out in these areas. A particularly monumental example of one of these altar-*podia* has recently been brought to light at the mound known as Tumulus II of the Sodo in Cortona. The custom of decorating the walls of the interior in fresco was very popular in the tombs of the better-off at Tarquinii. Artists of great ability along with more modest imitators painted scenes of dancing, banqueting and hunting on a layer of lime wash, handing down to posterity aspects of their client's life and customs. Other types of grave, common in Southern Etruria, i.e. in areas particularly rich in beds of tuff, were the so-called "cube" tombs. Taking their inspiration from houses as well as altars, they consist of a cubic block detached from the wall of rock behind and equipped with a carved door, often false, above which run friezes in relief reminiscent of altar decorations. The burial chamber, when not located inside the building, was constructed underneath it, completely below ground and accessible through a long, downward sloping passage. Arranged in several staggered rows, they created complexes of great scenic effect that necessarily required coordination by the city authorities, who were also responsible for assigning tombs to the various families.

Among the more unusual tombs of ancient Etruria there were a few, very rare ones of monumental appearance, where structures were provided to hold rituals in the open air. These probably commemorated people of particular importance – transformed into heroes with the passing of time – through games and performances representing their exploits: the tomb of the Cuccumella at Vulci contains a tiered space inside its very large mound that was used for theatrical performances. The intricate passages that run through this funeral

building recall another monumental tomb, that of King Porsenna at Chiusi: although never identified with certainty, we know of it from a complex description which Pliny the Elder took from Varro (*Natural History* XXXVI, 19). The model of construction, while considered a one-off, was akin to that of other structures for sacred and funeral use: in fact its form was similar, but on an infinitely larger scale, to that of the altars sometimes reproduced on the cinerary urns of Volterra, with a parallelepiped base surmounted by pyramids. (M.M.)

THE VALLEYS OF THE FIORA AND ALBEGNA

Areas frequented by humans since the remote past and characterized by natural scenery of surprising beauty, the fertile valleys of the Fiora and Albegna became vital means of communication between the coastal and inland regions during the Etruscan era. Navigable for much of its lower stretches, the Albegna River permitted the transport and diffusion of artifacts produced in the active "workshops" of Vulci or in the Mediterranean basin. The valley of the Fiora, with the important road that ran through it, connected the northern areas with the southern ones and the valley of the Tiber with the cities on the coast. This explains why its centers of habitation had close cultural affinities with Vulci as well as showing signs of significant influences from the area of Falerii and Capena.

Sovana

Opposite, a view of the sunken road of San Sebastiano at Sovana

View of the medieval burg

pp. 106-7: the complex of the Ildebranda Tomb, first half of the 3rd cent. BC

The fascinating medieval burg of Sovana stands on the site of the ancient city of Suana, a broad tufaceous plateau on the left bank of the Fiora frequented since the Bronze Age. Its development in the Orientalizing period was due to its strategic location on the important roads linking Vulci with Volsinii and inland Central Etruria. Long stretches of these have survived and are an impressive sight: called *cavoni*, they have steep walls cut out of the rock that can reach a height of 25 m.

Remains of the ancient city (6th cent. BC) have been uncovered in the area now occupied by the cathedral, while the ring of walls in *opus quadratum* seems to date from the following century. Suana experienced a new period of prosperity, ascribable to intense agricultural exploitation of the territory, at the end of the

4th cent. BC, when the urban center spread onto several parts of the plateau that had not previously been occupied. At the same time a fairly characteristic local production of handicrafts emerged, as is evident from the numerous terracotta votive offerings found in a sacred area near Via del Cavone (locally known as the *tagliata* or "cut").

The affluence attained by Suana in the Hellenistic era is reflected today by the monumental rupestrian necropolises that ring the city. At the end of Via del Cavone (which has Etruscan inscriptions on its walls) can be seen the *aedicula* tomb of the Typhon (4th cent. BC), which gets its name from an erroneous interpretation of the female figure adorning the central part of the carved *tympanum*, thought to be the sea monster's head. Further on, at the Poggio Felceto, stands the monumental Hildebrand Tomb, named after medieval Sovana's most famous citizen, the man who went on to become Pope Gregory VII. The imposing structure, datable to the first half of the 3rd

century, was constructed in the form of a temple on a high podium, adorned with six columns on the front and three on the short sides that support a coffered ceiling, and a rich sculptural decoration with fantastic animals on the tympanum. Continuing along a fascinating route through a place where the work of human beings and nature have fused with surprising effects, we come to several graves carved out of the tuff, including the Pola Tomb (mid-3rd cent. BC). It too is adorned with a majestic colonnaded portico, although unfortunately only part of this has survived. Another burial place of particular interest is located at Sopraripa, near the sunken road of Via di San Sebastiano. It is an *aedicula* called the tomb of the Siren (second half of the 3rd cent. BC), whose pediment is decorated with a sculpture of Scylla, the mythological creature that was half woman and half fish. In the niche underneath reclines the figure of the deceased.

Inner chamber of the Ildebranda Tomb

Bronze crockery from the Ildebranda Tomb, first half of the 3rd cent. BC. Museo Archeologico, Florence

The front of the tomb of the Siren in the necropolis of Sopraripa, second half of the 3rd cent. BC

Poggio Buco

View of some tombs from the 7th-6th cent. BC

Terracotta basin with figures and horsemen from Valle Rodeta near Pitigliano, second half of the 7th cent. BC. Museo Archeologico, Florence

Sparne had a sacred area in which clay architectural slabs adorned with figures of animals, scenes of departure on a cart and figures of warriors have been found. A number of dwellings and a paved road have also been brought to light. From the late period (2nd-1st cent. BC) dates a deposit of votive offerings made up of reproductions of parts of the anatomy, terracotta figures of animals and numerous Roman coins.

The necropolises of Poggio Buco are laid out in a ring around the Etruscan city and contain pit tombs, along with large chamber tombs with multiple burials from the Orientalizing period. Large amounts of Etruscan and Corinthian pottery and *bucchero* ware made in Vulci were found in the latter.

In a strategic position on the right bank of the Fiora stood an important Etruscan settlement that exercised control over a road linking the territory of Vulci with Volsinii and Clusium.

For a long time the ruins in this locality were believed to be those of the city called Statonia in the sources, on the grounds of the discovery of several pieces of shot (a sort of projectile generally made out of lead) inscribed with the word Staties, but this is now thought to have been the name of the manufacturer.

The ancient center located on the hill of Le

Castro

Further south, only 20 km from Vulci, stood another important Etruscan center, occupying the high ground between the Olpeta and Monache rivers, tributaries of the Fiora, on the site where medieval Castro would later be built. Destroyed in 1649 by the troops of Pope Innocent X during his struggle with the powerful Farnese family, nothing remains of the burg but a few vestiges overgrown with vegetation.

It has been suggested that this settlement was the city of Statonia, mentioned in the sources for the presence of good building stone on its territory, among other reasons. The hypothesis is supported by the fact that Pliny and

Seneca refer to a lake in the vicinity of the city, which could plausibly be identified with the small body of water called Mezzano.

Several of the tombs discovered so far, which include well, pit, chest and chamber types, appear to have been very rich. One of them, the tomb of the Biga, contained a rare two-horse chariot decorated with bronze plate that is now in the Museo di Villa Giulia. The tomb of the Bronzes, with its rich "princely" contents, had a lavish ornamentation with sculptures of lions, sphinxes and rams produced in Vulci in the first half of the 6th cent. BC.

Saturnia

Dionysius of Halicarnassus describes the Etruscan Urina as one of the oldest cities in Italy, founded by the mythical people of the Pelasgi. Excavations have revealed traces of frequentation of the site as far back as the Late Bronze Age (10th cent. BC), although the earliest significant archeological evidence dates from the 8th century.

The city owed much of its growth to the advantages of its position at the confluence of the Stellata and Albegna, and its control of the important road that ran along the valley of the same name and linked the territory of Vulci with that of Volsinii, as well as the Amiata area and Clusium.

The remains of a platform built out of slabs of tuff and bounded on one side by wooden

A chamber tomb in the necropolis of the Puntone

The Porta Romana with a view of the Via Clodia

columns have been uncovered in the old settlement. It may have been located next to a sacred building, judging by a number of fragments of architectural slabs from the second half of the 4th cent. BC that seem to have been derived from Volsinian models. The evidence from the vast cemeteries surrounding the city is much more substantial. Well tombs have been found at the locality of Sede di Carlo, while the necropolises at Pian di Palma and Puntone, on the right bank of the Albegna, have yielded pit, chamber and partition tombs that were in use between the second quarter of the 7th cent. BC and the middle of the 5th.

The conquest of Vulci by the Romans in 280 BC must have wreaked a great deal of destruction on the settlement of Urina as well. It became the seat of a prefecture over the following decades, following a model of organization adopted by Rome in the regions it conquered by force. The city was given new impetus by the opening of the Via Clodia which connected it with Rome. In 183 BC a colony called Saturnia was founded there by the city's triumviri and then, like other Etruscan centers, laid waste during the civil war between Marius and Sulla that raged in Etruria around 80 BC.

Ghiaccio Forte

The settlement at Ghiaccio Forte, located on an elevation to the north of the Albegna River, was only discovered in 1972. Emerging in the 4th cent. BC on a site already frequented in the Archaic period, it covered an area of 4 hectares and was surrounded by a ring of walls built out of stone splinters topped with unfired bricks that must have reached a height of at least 6 m and stretched for almost 1 km. Access to the settlement was through three gates of monumental appearance with vestibules, constructed from blocks of travertine and nenfro and rough stones of large size. Vestiges of the cobbled paving of the roads and drainage channels for meteoric water have been found near them.

A sacred area must have been located on the western side of the hill, and already been in use in the late Archaic period, judging by a deposit of anatomical ex-votos in terracotta and bronze statuettes of people making offerings and animals. These would have satisfied the religious needs of a modestly prosperous population that relied on farming. The settlement also comprised a very large dwelling that has been identified as the residence of the Statie family: numerous pieces of shot stamped with their device have been found in various places in the valleys of the Albegna and Fiora. The family must have played a primary role in the defense of this part of the territory of Vulci against the advance of the Romans. There is also evidence for the presence of Celtic warriors at Ghiaccio Forte, in the form of a sword found near the southeast gate.

The destruction of the settlement in the early decades of the 3rd century has to be ascribed to the Roman army, engaged in the conquest of Vulci.

Magliano

Numerous graves have been found in the hilly territory bounded by the courses of the Albegna and Osa rivers, which in the Roman era belonged to the colony of Heba, mentioned by Ptolemy. They were connected with isolated huts, like the one unearthed at Poggio alle Sorche, or with small farming villages, evidently under the control of Vulci.

The two partition tombs with paintings on their walls discovered at the localities of Le Ficaie (now lost) and, much more recently, Cancellone are to be ascribed to members of the landowning aristocracy. In an extraordinary state of preservation, the latter is decorated with fantastic animals in the Orientalizing style dating from the late 7th cent. BC. A disk of lead (5th-4th cent. BC) with inscriptions engraved in a spiral on both sides that appear to be formulas of dedication to gods of the underworld and the heavens seems to be related to a later burial ground at Santa Maria in Borraccia.

Lead disk with inscription from Santa Maria in Borraccia near Magliano, 5th-4th cent. BC. Museo Archeologico, Florence

Marsiliana d'Albegna

Terracotta votive heads from the Marsiliana area. Museo Archeologico e d'Arte della Maremma, Grosseto

Ivory tablet with alphabet engraved on the edge from the Circle of the Ivories, Marsiliana, 675-650 BC. Museo Archeologico, Florence

The settlement at Marsiliana d'Albegna can hypothetically be identified as Caletra, the town in whose territory Livy and Pliny the Elder say the Roman colony of Saturnia was founded. The locality is about 13 km from the sea and its flowering in the Orientalizing period (7th cent. BC) may be explained by the relative navigability of the last stretch of the Albegna, which would have favored trade in products arriving by sea.

Scanty clues as to the location of the ancient settlement have been brought to light at Uliveto di Bandinella, a short distance from the Castello Corsini at Marsiliana, while the necropolises have yielded materials of great importance. The best known cemetery is the one at Banditella, where around a hundred tombs have been excavated. Mostly of the pit type and all with an east-west orientation, some are surrounded by circles of stones in a form of burial that is well documented at Vetulonia. The contents of the Circle of the Ivories (675-650 BC) were particularly rich, comprising among other things a set of writing materials made up of a famous ivory tablet with the alphabet engraved along the upper edge, two *styli* and two scrapers, reflecting the rank of its owner. The man buried in the circle of the Fibula also enjoyed great prestige: near the pit tomb with its rich grave goods a paved area has been excavated in which implements for cooking meat, pots for the consumption of wine and weapons had been deposited, with the intention of underlining the role played by the deceased in society. There are also some particularly sumptuous burials in the necropolis of the Perazzetta, where carts have been found in the tombs. The contrast between the opulence of the 7th-century graves and the modesty of the later ones has suggested a progressive decline of the settlement that would lead to its abandonment in the second half of the 6th cent. BC.

Doganella

An Etruscan center of considerable importance, which can be identified as the Kalousion mentioned by Polybius in connection with the battle between Romans and Gauls at Telamon (225 BC), stood on the right bank of the Patrignone in the vicinity of Doganella. The old settlement had a long ring of walls that was totally destroyed in 1842 when a road was constructed to link Magliano with the salt pans at Bocca d'Albegna. Several buildings datable to between the 6th and 4th cent. BC have been uncovered in the urban area. The town was destroyed sometime between the late 4th cent. BC and the early 3rd and no longer frequented.

Talamone

Comprehensive reconstruction of the pediment of the temple on Talamonaccio, 150-130 BC. Museo Civico, Orbetello

pp. 114-15: details of the pediment on Talamonaccio with, on the left, Adrastus on his chariot and, right, Amphiaraus descending with his chariot into the Underworld. Museo Civico, Orbetello

Two views of the remains of the temple on Talamonaccio

The hill of Talamonaccio, rising high above the sea and dominating the mouth of the Osa River and the roadstead of Bengodi, on whose shores the port must have been located, played a significant role in the control of sea routes in the Tyrrhenian. Excavations of the locality, frequented as early as the Chalcolithic, have yielded materials from the Late Bronze Age and the Iron Age, but it does not seem to have been permanently occupied until the 4th cent. BC. Older finds (6th cent. BC) have been made on the neighboring hill of Bengodi, including the remains of architectural terracottas and pottery. The settlement on Talamonaccio had a double circle of walls that were destroyed in the 19th century. At the same time damage was inflicted on the well-known sanctuary built at the end of the 4th century BC, of which parts of the foundations and the podium are visible today. Its prosperity derived from agricultural exploitation of the hinterland and a flourishing mercantile activity, for which evidence is provided by some materials uncovered in the necropolis situated at the foot of the hill, including fine bronze artifacts dating from the 4th cent. BC.

Telamon, as it was called by the Romans, is mentioned in the literature as the site of the defeat inflicted on the Gauls in 225 BC by the Roman army under the command of consuls Lucius Emilius Papus and Gaius Attilius Regulus. Several burials of men and horses discovered at the locality of Camporegio have been linked with the battle. Later the city's name appears in connection with the return of Tiberius Sempronius Gracchus from Numantia and again in 87 BC as the place where Marius landed on his way back from Africa. Five years later the settlement and the surrounding territory would be sacked by Sulla.

The most celebrated monument excavated in this area is undoubtedly the terracotta pediment from the 2nd cent. BC (on display at Orbetello) that adorned the sanctuary on the hill of Talamonaccio. It represents the myth of the Seven against Thebes with, at the center, the fratricidal struggle between Eteocles and Polyneices in front of Oedipus. This may have been an allusion to the strong social tensions sparked off by the Roman conquest. (G.P.)

Roads and Means of Transport

I As early as the Copper and Bronze Ages the populations of Central Italy had a high degree of mobility on land, a fact to which the spread of particular categories of goods to remote areas a long way from the coast bears witness. Even though journeys were made solely on foot and with beasts of burden, distances of hundreds and hundreds of kilometers were covered both for transhumance and for purposes of trade. Transhumance, a typical phenomenon of the Middle Bronze Age but one that survived almost to our own day, even if only in marginal form, was in fact linked to the constant need for new areas for the grazing of flocks of sheep. From the cool summer pastures in the highlands, where the vegetation remained plentiful during the dry season, shepherds descended to the coastal plains in the fall, utilizing paths along the ridges wherever possible, rather than the swampy valley bottoms that were not always easily passable. The endpoints of these routes, or the stopping places along the way, often became centers of habitation which, favored by their concomitant role of crossroads and trading post, underwent rapid and early development. Some of these centers remained vital even with the advent of the Iron Age, notwithstanding the drastic reduction in sheep farming during that period in favor of the more sedentary raising of pigs and cattle (as the remains of animals found in various excavations attest), and the consequent scaling down of transhumance.

In addition, the development of mining and a growing production of handicrafts favored forms of manufacturing linked to particular areas and fixed infrastructures. This meant that the need for movement was connected more with the transport of raw materials and manufactured products, and the routes followed were not necessarily the traditional ones of transhumance. So a new network of communications between the inland areas and the coast and between north and south began to take shape, resulting in the decline of some localities and the birth of new settlements.

Over the following centuries roads assumed an increasingly important role and the maintenance of their practicability, once dependent on the periodical passage of travelers, became a responsibility of the communities. In some cases these carried out structural works, paving the roads with cobbles or, wherever the nature of the ground permitted, cutting them directly into the rock. In the region of Viterbo, for example, some old towns and villages are still surrounded by a grid of so-called "cuts," i.e. roads sunk deep in

The Cavone at Sovana, Etruscan road cut into the tuff

Reconstruction of the *carpentum* faced with bronze plate from Corciano, Perugia, second half of the 6th cent. BC. Museo Archeologico, Perugia

the tuff, usually open to the sky but sometimes with stretches of tunnel. Although today they look like simple trenches cut in the ground, their appearance in ancient times was very different, and in certain cases — as at Norchia — they were paved with wooden boards set on ties and flanked by a ditch to collect rainwater. Given their narrowness, some of them must have been one-way streets, suggesting the involvement of public institutions in the planning of the routes of access and exit and in the maintenance of the roads. Of great interest has been the recent identification, at Capannori (Lucca), of a stretch of cobbled paving belonging to the "highway of the two seas" from the Archaic Etruscan era:

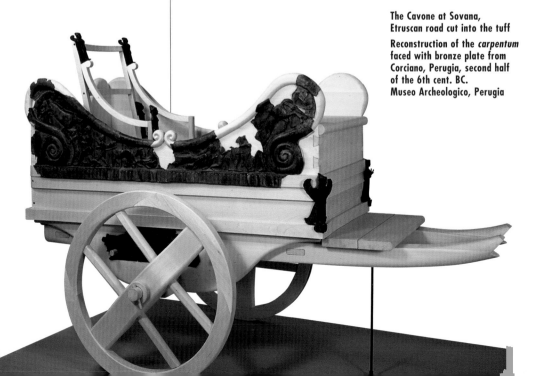

Facing slab with chariots
and warriors from
Colombella near Praeneste,
first half of the 6th cent. BC.
Museo Nazionale Etrusco
di Villa Giulia, Rome

according to the ancient literary
sources, this road allowed people to
travel from the Tyrrhenian to the
Adriatic in just three days.
Along these and other routes moved
armies, farmers, pilgrims and
merchants, often in caravans whose
appearance has been preserved by the
Perugian "Sperandio Sarcophagus,"
which may represent the return from a
military expedition. The men, on foot,
are accompanied by donkeys loaded
with goods and chattels, while other
objects are carried on the backs of slaves
walking in single file, bound together by
their necks so that they could not escape.
The presence of several armed men may
allude to the existence of bandits, the
equivalent on land of the equally
widespread piracy on the seas.
Journeys were also made by cart,
generally with just two wheels. The
oldest of these, in use between the
Villanovan and Orientalizing periods
and all the way up to Archaic times,
were very light models intended

principally for military use. They were
an article of great luxury first for the
principes and then for the aristocratic
elite, retaining a high economic and
symbolic value. Unlike these elegant
chariots with a small wooden body
adorned with sheets of decorated
bronze, the larger vehicles used by
farmers were much plainer, with
bodywork and sideboards made out of
simple slanting poles fixed to the
frame, as a small votive model from
Bolsena shows. The wheels were solid
and to the shaft, in all likelihood, was
yoked a pair of oxen, better suited by
their strength to the slow transport of
heavy loads.
Another two-wheeled vehicle was a cart
with spoked wheels resembling a gig,
common in Etruria and the Italic area
from the 8th-7th cent. BC up until the
beginning of the 5th, on which people
could travel seated on a small box with
their feet resting on a suspended
board, while the longitudinal bars of
the frame converged at the top in a

characteristic trident-shaped end piece.
Similar to the typical traditional sledge
– or *travois* – of the Apennines, from
which it differed by the presence of
wheels, this cart appears to have been
used by women as well. Indeed it was
sometimes placed in their tombs, as
was the *carpentum*, the vehicle in which
tradition has it that Tarquinius Priscus
arrived in Rome with his Etruscan wife
Tanaquil. This typical two-wheeled cart
with quadrangular bodywork and
sideboards had a small box for the
driver and one passenger; the seat and
space for the load were covered with an
awning, supported by curved ribs and
held in place by crisscrossed ties. Very
common in the Hellenistic period, it is
frequently represented on cinerary
urns, such as the ones in Volterra, as
the vehicle used to make the last
journey into the afterlife. (M.M.)

Etruscan urn with covered *carpentum*
from Volterra, 2nd cent. BC. Museo
Etrusco Guarnacci, Volterra

"Sperandio Sarcophagus,"
detail of the relief with
columns of soldiers returning
from war, early 5th cent. BC.
Museo Archeologico, Perugia

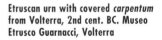

THE MAJOR CENTERS
OF THE TUSCAN COAST

Still an area of great scenic beauty, the strip of coast extending to the north of the Argentario as far as the promontory of Piombino was a very difficult environment in antiquity, characterized by broad areas of marshland and pools of water. Yet it had been frequented since the Paleolithic, as finds made in the territory have shown, and was open to outside influences as well, thanks to the easy landfalls offered by the numerous lagoons. They provided shelter for the ships carrying foreign goods to Etruria and iron ore from Elba, for smelting in the furnaces of Baratti.

Populonia

Opposite, the necropolis of the Grottoes with the bay of Baratti

The tomb of the Cylindrical Boxes in the necropolis of San Cerbone; below, the tomb of the Flabella in the Porcareccia Necropolis

Founded, according to the ancient sources, either by peoples from Corsica or by Volterrans, Populonia was the only large Etruscan city built on the sea, overlooking the splendid bay of Baratti. Its old name of Pupluna or Fufluna reveals a close connection with Fufluns, the Etruscan god of wine and equivalent of the Greek Dionysus and Roman Bacchus.

From the outset, Populonia's great prosperity was dependent on exploitation of the mineral deposits in the Campigliese hills behind the city and on the island of Elba. Several of the burial grounds (Poggio del Telegrafo, San Cerbone, Casone) that extend over the reliefs and plateaus facing onto the gulf of Baratti date from the oldest phase (9th cent. BC), while the area of the promontory on which the city was to rise must have already been occupied by a village at this time. The tombs, of the well type, have yielded decorated biconical cinerary urns and a few hut urns, accompanied by modest grave goods made up chiefly of objects of personal use. In this period a number of finds of pottery and bronze artifacts already indicate contacts with Sardinia, which must have favored an early development of metallurgy through the acquisition of more sophisticated smelting techniques.

In the Orientalizing period the necropolises of Populonia were characterized by large burial mounds, each with a circular drum of stone surrounded by paving and a very low *dromos* providing access to a quadrangular chamber covered with a mock dome. The only rite used appears to have been that of inhumation, with the bodies laid out on stone beds adorned with shapely legs, as can be seen in the tombs of the Carts and the Funeral Beds in particular. The first of these tumuli is the most

The tomb of the Chariots in the necropolis of San Cerbone

Small bronze representing *Ajax committing suicide* from the tumulus of the Funeral Beds in the Casone Necropolis, 480-460 BC. Museo Archeologico, Florence

imposing in the necropolis of San Cerbone and takes its name from its extraordinary contents, a racing chariot and a carriage resembling a gig. The tumulus of the Funeral Beds (necropolis of the Casone), whose ceiling has collapsed, is smaller and contained a bronze figure of *Ajax Committing Suicide*. Rich burials of this kind, which include the tomb of the Flabella (named after its large fans made of embossed bronze) and the tomb of the Jewelry, excavated in the necropolis of the Porcareccia, can be ascribed to members of a ruling class of the "princely" type whose wealth derived from control of the mining industry and maritime trade.

From the late 6th cent. BC onward *aedicula* tombs were built in the necropolis of the Casone. The best-preserved example, named after the bronze statue of a man making an offering that was found in it, must have had an elaborately decorated roof, adorned with stone sculptures. The tomb is surrounded by other burials inside stone chests that are an indication of the existence of clans based on ties of kinship.

During this period, as in subsequent ones, the territory of Populonia does not appear to have been particularly large: inland it extended to the Campigliese hills, where copper, lead, tin, silver and iron ore was mined. Settlements connected with the extractive industry must have been located on Monte Pitti, while the remains of furnaces for the roasting of ore and kilns for the firing of pottery have been found in the area of Madonna di Fucinaia. Their date is uncertain but they may go back as far as the 5th century, judging by sev-

Aedicula **tomb of the Small Bronze of a Man Making an Offering in the Casone Necropolis**

On the left, the tomb of the Jewelry; right, the excavations of the acropolis

eral miner's lamps found in the production structures, which were abandoned before the 3rd cent. BC, when the zone was utilized as a burial ground. Populonia had close ties with the island of Elba, where the iron ore underwent a first stage of roasting before being shipped to the city on the coast. In fact a huge "industrial" district already existed a short distance from the port of Baratti in the 6th cent. BC, where the Etruscan artisans engaged in the production of iron worked and lived, while the residences of the wealthy aristocracy were concentrated on the top of the hill.

A sure sign of Populonia's affluence is provided by the minting (middle of the 5th cent. BC) of several series of silver coins, decorated with figures of the Chimera or Hermes, along with a series of gold coins with lion's heads.

Remains of the industrial area on the Porcareccia hillock; opposite, the necropolis of the Grottoes

Subsequently coins were struck with heads of the Gorgon or Athena and the city's name on the reverse. The florid economic situation lasted into the 4th century, as is evident from the graves in the necropolis of the Grotte, subterranean chambers arranged on several levels and located inside disused sandpits. It was at this locality that the only two chambers with a painted decoration were discovered, called the tombs of the Ogee and the Dolphins on the basis of the ornamentation of their walls.

Around the middle of the 3rd cent. BC the city entered the political orbit of Rome, but Populonia's continued involvement in mining is demonstrated by its supply of iron (205 BC) to Scipio for the expedition against Hannibal.

The dominant feature in the panorama of the upper city is the so-called building of the Logge, where a mosaic was found depicting marine scenes filled with a great variety of fish. More recently another mosaic has been uncovered with Negroid figures that seem to derive from Alexandrine models.

Following the civil war between Marius and Sulla a period of deep crisis commenced for Populonia as well. This was described at the end of the 1st century by the geographer Strabo, who records a certain amount of activity still going in the port area and mentions the existence of several sanctuaries and a few other constructions in the urban center. On the shore, on the other hand, stood a number of luxurious villas like the one partially excavated at Poggio del Molino.

Vetulonia

The entrance passage of the Pietrera Tumulus, 630-600 BC

Bronze incense boat of Sardinian manufacture from the tomb of the Dux, mid-7th cent. BC. Museo Archeologico, Florence

Vetulonia (Vetluna or Vatluna in Etruscan) has been identified with the locality of Colonna di Buriano ever since the sensational discoveries made by Isidoro Falchi from 1880 onward. In 1887 a royal decree was issued restoring the prestigious name of the Etruscan city to the village in the Tuscan Maremma. According to an ancient tradition it was from Vetulonia that Rome took its insignia of power: the lictor's fasces, the curule chair, the red-bordered toga and the war trumpet. The city appears on the so-called *Throne of Claudius* (a sculpture from the imperial age found at Cerveteri and now in the Museo Lateranense, Rome), providing evidence of a clear vocation for mercantile activity, carried out through one or more ports that must have exploited, like the neighboring city

of Rusellae, the basin of the lagoon formed by the Prile. Covering what is now the plain of Castiglione, this deep and navigable lake connected with the sea dried up over the course of the centuries, partly as a result of drainage activities.

While little is known so far about the proto-Villanovan phase of occupation of the territory, that of the Iron Age (9th-8th cent. BC) is well documented, especially by the materials found in the necropolis of Poggio alla Guardia. The well tombs, only rarely containing more than one burial, have yielded biconical ossuaries and a large number of hut urns that already reflect the diversification of a society whose wealth was based on exploitation of the deposits of metal ore in the Massetano.

The refinement of the techniques used for the extraction and working of metals in the Orientalizing period brought a marked growth in the population and economy of Vetulonia, amply documented by extraordinary finds in the necropolises. This was the time when circle tombs appeared. Consisting of one or more pits inside a circle of stones, they contained

sumptuous grave goods, including objects imported from Syria, Cypress and Egypt, along
with artifacts from Sardinia like bronze incense boats. From Southern Etruria, on the
other hand, came fine objects made of silver.
This economic and cultural fervor gave rise to
a refined local craft industry, specializing in
the working of bronze (vases and tripods with
handles shaped like lotus flowers, incense
burners, stands for pots) and gold. The tech-

niques of granulation, dusting and embossing
were used to turn the latter into precious jewelry and ornaments, now on display at the
Museo Archeologico in Florence.

In the second half of the 7th century the
"princely" class of Vetulonia utilized monumental *tholos* tombs, covered by mounds of
earth with conical pillars on top, long *dromoi*
of access and central pillars supporting corbel
vaults. An example of this type is the Pietrera

Excavations of the
Hellenistic residential
district known as the
"Scavi di Città"

Chamber tomb of Poggio
Pelliccia in the necropolis
of Giuncarico; below, the
restored interior of the
tomb of the Little Devil II

Tomb (630-600 BC), located inside a mound with a diameter of over 60 m and height of 14. A broad *dromos* with two small cells at the sides led to a chamber that must have collapsed shortly after its construction and then had another tomb built on top of it. Rich grave goods have been found in the vicinity, along with eight fragmentary stone statues possibly representing the ancestors of the deceased that may have decorated the access corridor. An-

other large tomb was the contemporary one of the Little Devil II. Recently restored, it has been subjected to new excavations that have brought to light parts of stone funeral beds similar to those of the Pietrera, along with numerous objects. The nearby tomb of the Gold Fibula has similar structural characteristics, but is on a more modest scale.

The territory of Vetulonia must have comprised the coastal belt between Castiglione della Pescaia and Pian d'Alma, where some necropolises have been uncovered (Val Berretta and Pian d'Alma), and the rich mining area of Massa Marittima. Settlements were located along the roads that ran through the valleys of the Bruna and its tributary the Sovata, and on the route to Massa Marittima. Here stands the monumental tumulus of Poggio Pelliccia, which has a *tholos* tomb with a quadrangular chamber at its center and two pit burials on its slopes. Although it was looted in antiquity, the contents of the tomb, now in the Museo Civico of Vetulonia, include fine Corinthian and Greek-Oriental pottery that indicates the tomb was in use between the middle of the 7th and the middle of the 5th cent. BC. The great importance of this route is confirmed by the burial grounds of Selvello and the Torraccia.

The oldest remains of Etruscan Vetluna have been identified in some stretches of the walls in *opus siliceum* ("Mura dell'Arce") dating from the late 6th to 5th cent. BC, visible

Terracotta slab from the Hellenistic period with Creusa bathing, from the excavations of Vetulonia. Museo Civico Archeologico "Isidoro Falchi," Vetulonia

almost in the center of the modern town and at the locality of Piantoni. Remains of a sacred deposit of votive offerings dating from sometime between the 6th and 5th century have been unearthed in the archeological area of Costa Murata, providing evidence for a continuity of life in the settlement that has been confirmed by other finds from the Hellenistic era.

A residential district dating from the 3rd-1st cent. BC and known as the "Scavi di Città" has been brought to light at Poggiarello Renzetti. Destroyed in all likelihood by a fire, it is traversed by a paved street, the *decumanus*, on to which face several storehouses and houses with *atria*. In one of these, which has been completely excavated, there was a lavish decoration of clay reliefs representing scenes from the myth of Medea.

Other urbanized areas have been excavated at the localities of Apparita and Costa dei Lippi, and here too a stretch of paved road and parts of buildings decorated with architectural terracottas have been uncovered. Coins in silver and bronze, some of them inscribed with the word *Vatl* (Vatluna), the Etruscan name of the city, were probably issued in the closing decades of the 4th and the initial ones of the 3rd cent. BC.

Like many of the Etruscan centers, Vetulonia entered the Roman orbit over the course of the 3rd century, perhaps peacefully. But it always had a marginal role, to the extent that some of the sources call it an *oppidum*, or outpost. In 89 BC it was assigned to the Scaptia tribe and the few people who still lived there became Roman citizens.

Accesa

In the vicinity of the small lake of Accesa, just over 7 km from Massa Marittima, the remains of an Etruscan town dating from between the late 7th and the 6th cent. BC have been identified. Although still partly under excavation, an area has been equipped with facilities for visitors.

The development of the settlement has been connected with exploitation of the deposits of copper pyrites and silver-bearing galena (valuable raw materials used to make bronze that were much in demand in antiquity), in which the zone is particularly rich. The dwellings brought to light so far are arranged in groups characterized by the presence of a large building surrounded by smaller ones, something that may well reflect the emergence of a social system which already tended to emphasize the role of a dominant class. All that remains of the various structures are the foundations of rough-hewn stones, quarried locally, while no trace has survived of the upper part, built out of perishable material. Tools used in the household activities of women, such as weights and spindle whorls for weaving and spinning, have been found inside them, along with numerous pots for dining and cooking. Small groups of burials, with pit, chest and chamber tombs, are located a short distance away. The discovery of well tombs indicates that the zone was already occupied in the 8th century, even through there is no unambiguous evidence for settled areas in this period. Even the oldest of the finds suggest a strong cultural dependence on Vetulonia, only 15 km away from Accesa and linked with it by an easy route through the valley of the Bruna.

**Boot-shaped impasto
vase from tomb 14 at
Accesa Lake, second half
of the 8th cent. BC.
Museo Archeologico,
Massa Marittima**

**Large impasto *kantharos*
from tomb 12 at Accesa
Lake, second half of the
7th cent. BC.
Museo Archeologico,
Massa Marittima**

Roselle

The city spread over two hills facing the former basin of the Prile, a large lagoon connected with the sea that has now almost completely dried up, where Rusellae, as the Romans called it, had a port. The zone was already frequented in protohistoric times, when the elevation of the Poggio Moscona, above the future Etruscan city, must have been the location of a Bronze-Age settlement. Vestiges of the Villanovan period (9th-8th cent. BC) have been found at Nomadelfia, where a small necropolis from the Early Iron Age has been excavated.

By the middle of the 7th century the city already had a ring of walls built of unfired brick, and remains of residential structures with earthen floors and constructed from sun-dried clay can be dated to the same period. The oldest of these constructions are the "house of the enclosure" and the "house with two rooms," which may have had an important public function for the community as they were not altered in any way even in the Roman era.

The flourishing of Roselle, although it never attained the level of luxury and wealth of Vetulonia, must have been based on farm-

Right, well curb, 6th cent. BC., and below, *olla* and cooking stove, 6th cent. BC. from the house of the Impluvium. Museo Archeologico e d'Arte della Maremma, Grosseto

Below, impasto ossuary from the necropolis of Nomadelfia, 8th-7th cent. BC. Museo Archeologico e d'Arte della Maremma, Grosseto

ing of the highly fertile plain below (on the southeast shore of the Prile) and the control of important means of communication, such as the one that passed through the nearby valley of the Ombrone.

Over the course of the 6th century the city was given a new and massive ring of walls: preserved almost in its entirety, it ran for over 3 km and enclosed two hills. Reaching a height of 5 m in some places, the walls were built with the technique of *opus siliceum*, using blocks of very large size cut from the northern side of the hill of Roselle, as the remains of the terracing of the ancient quarries testify. Several gates have been identified in the walls at points corresponding to the roads that connected the city with the north, with the area of Monte Amiata and with the south of Etruria. Along these routes were located several necropolises with burial mounds and chamber tombs roofed with corbel vaults. A number of

View of the Roman forum looking toward the southern hill

tombs have also been excavated in the necropolis of Case di Mota.

The large house of the *impluvium*, covering an area of about 300 sq. m, can be dated to the same period as the construction of the walls. The building, approximately square in plan, was laid out around a covered courtyard communicating with eight other rooms, including one paved with clay panels that housed a basin to collect rainwater.

The archeological finds suggest a continuity of inhabitation in the 5th and 4th centuries as well, before Roselle came into conflict with Rome and suffered a heavy defeat (298 BC). Four years later, according to Livy, it was be-

sieged and finally conquered by the consul Lucius Postumius Megellus, who laid waste to the territory and took a large number of prisoners.

The *Lex Julia* and the successive *Lex Plautia-Papiria* granted Roman citizenship to the inhabitants of Roselle, who were enrolled in the Roman tribe Arnensis, but it was not until much later that the city was given the status of a colony, documented by several inscriptions and the literary sources. Its subsequent decline is recorded by the Latin poet Rutilius Namatianus, who in the 5th century AD described it as semi-deserted, with large parts completely abandoned. Notwithstanding this slow decline, it remained a bishop's see until 1138.

The remains of the Etruscan period were partly covered up by the boom in building during the Roman era, when the massive structures still visible today were erected, but targeted excavations beneath them have made it possible to bring the oldest vestiges to light. On the top of the northern hill is set the elliptical amphitheater, part of it standing on the ruins of a house from the Hellenistic period (3rd-2nd cent. BC). The site overlooks the whole area of the forum, the heart of Roman Rusellae where much of the city's life went on. A paved street identified as the *cardo maximus*, with clear traces of ruts caused by the passage of carts, runs along the eastern side of the forum. It was interrupted at the point where the basilica stood and transformed into the *decumanus*, an unusual feature that may have been dictated by the topography of the valley.

Near the forum stood a construction with walls in *opus reticulatum*, the seat of the college of priests known as the *Falmines Augustales*, in which an important series of statues (now on show in Grosseto) has been found. They represent the emperor Claudius, his wife Livia and other members of the imperial family, who were evidently venerated here. A short distance away a huge *domus* with an *atrium*, heating system and numerous mosaic floors has been uncovered. From it come marble portraits of Emperor Tiberius, Agrippina the Elder and Drusus the Younger. Another group of

six statues was found in a building with an apse and niches in the walls located on the northwest side of the forum, while on the eastern side, beyond the *cardo maximus*, stood the basilica in which economic activities were carried out and justice was administered. Numerous shops lined the northern side of the *decumanus*. Further on are visible the remains of a huge central building with a *piscina*, whose site was occupied in the 5th century AD by a church and a cemetery with chest tombs. (G.P.)

The Roman amphitheater and, below, a view of the buildings from the Roman period near the *cardo maximus*

Techniques of Goldsmithry

While the earliest examples of objects made out of gold date from the Villanovan period, it was not until the Orientalizing phase that the Etruscans developed sophisticated techniques for working the material and genuine masterpieces were created. In fact the evolution of society, with the consequent emergence of an aristocracy, increased the demand for precious ornaments, which was initially met by imports from the Eastern Mediterranean. Later on, as this demand grew, a number of Oriental goldsmiths chose to move to the Italian peninsula. They would stay for long periods in the centers of residence of their clients, bringing a hitherto unknown store of technical know-how and a figurative repertoire that spread rapidly, partly with the help of local apprentices, and soon became distinctive features of Etruscan civilization himself.

Thus the gold *fibulae* from the Villanovan period that have occasionally come to light gave way to a vast range of brooches, earrings, necklaces, hairpins and bracelets for women, as well as *fibulae* and clasps used to fasten men's clothing. Among the more unusual and rare pieces are large hanging pectorals, oval or rectangular in shape. To these personal ornaments should be added the various types of precious gold or silver plate used for the banquet, one of the most important social rituals for the elite of the time.

The 6th century brought a change in taste, partly in relation to the growing crisis in the institution of monarchy and the consequent shift in the control of worship away from the *rex*, and therefore from the palace of the *princeps*, to the priests.

As a result the wealthier classes were more inclined to fund the construction of shrines and public works, providing them with the greatest return in terms of "image," while goldsmith's workshops, perhaps in part as a result of sumptuary laws (i.e. measures to limit the display of luxury), appear to have become less common in this period. As early as the 5th century, however, lavish forms of adornment returned under the influence of Oriental-Greek fashions, with new forms – such as rings with elliptical settings and studded earrings – and new ornamental motifs, enriched by the use of precious stones. But the greatest variety of forms and decorations would be attained in the Hellenistic period, when jewelry took on a stylistic richness that was almost baroque.

The oldest Etruscan gold work was characterized by the techniques of granulation and dusting. In fact the technical perfection of these objects made them almost unique, even though the methods were already in widespread use in the Middle East from the 2nd millennium BC onward. The custom of adorning the surface of jewelry by "granulation," i.e. applying tiny balls of gold with a diameter of around three tenths of a millimeter, may have reached the coasts of Etruria from Syria. The use of smaller particles, only a tenth of a millimeter in diameter and thus not distinguishable by the naked eye, constituted the basis of the "dusting" technique. These microscopic granules were produced by the fusion of little squares of gold leaf and powdered carbon in a heated crucible. They were then graded by size and attached by the goldsmith to the surface of the jewelry by means of an organic glue (called *santerna* by Pliny). Subsequently they would be permanently fixed by heating with copper salts.

Most pieces of Etruscan jewelry were not solid castings, but made out of plates of gold decorated in relief. The objects were often composed of two halves joined together to form a piece in the round, hollow on the inside. Thus the preliminary work of the goldsmith was to beat the material, in order to produce thin sheets of constant thickness. These were then cut

Gold earring with granulation and head of a Black man in amber, from Volterra, 3rd cent. BC. Museo Etrusco Guarnacci, Volterra

into the required shape with a chisel or a skiving knife, for Etruscan goldsmiths did not use shears. At this point two different procedures were followed, depending on the design of the object. In the case of a relief decoration with a repeated motif, a bronze punch was made and the design stamped from the back. When the design only appeared once, on the other hand, a preparatory outline of the pattern was engraved on the outside of the sheet with straight chisels, while the parts to be represented in relief were embossed from the rear with rounded chisels.

A magnificent example of Etruscan gold work, as well as an extraordinary synthesis of the various techniques employed, is provided by the pectoral from the Bernardini Tomb at Praeneste that is now in the Museo di Villa Giulia in Rome. Perhaps made at Caere by craftsmen trained in the Syrian-Phoenician style, this exceptional object was created around 670 BC and its small surface area (17 x 10 cm) is adorned with a total of 131 animals in full relief (lions, chimeras, sirens, horses), embossed on thin plates of gold and then set between three cylinders. The ones at the ends are finely decorated with a granulation of meanders. (M.M.)

Opposite, detail of the large pectoral from the Bernardini Tomb at Praeneste, second quarter of the 7th cent. BC. Museo Nazionale Etrusco di Villa Giulia, Rome

Leech-shaped fibula from the tomb of the Lictor at Vetulonia, second half of the 7th cent. BC. and, dragon-shaped fibula from Marsiliana, second quarter of the 7th cent. BC. Museo Archeologico, Florence

Necklace with pendants from the tomb of the Silver Lions at Vetulonia, second half of the 7th cent. BC. Museo Civico Archeologico "Isidoro Falchi," Vetulonia

Pair of earrings from the Badia Necropolis at Volterra, mid-4th cent. BC. Museo Etrusco Guarnacci, Volterra

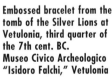

Embossed bracelet from the tomb of the Silver Lions at Vetulonia, third quarter of the 7th cent. BC. Museo Civico Archeologico "Isidoro Falchi," Vetulonia

Kotyle from the Bernardini Tomb at Praeneste, second quarter of the 7th cent. BC. Museo Nazionale Etrusco di Villa Giulia, Rome

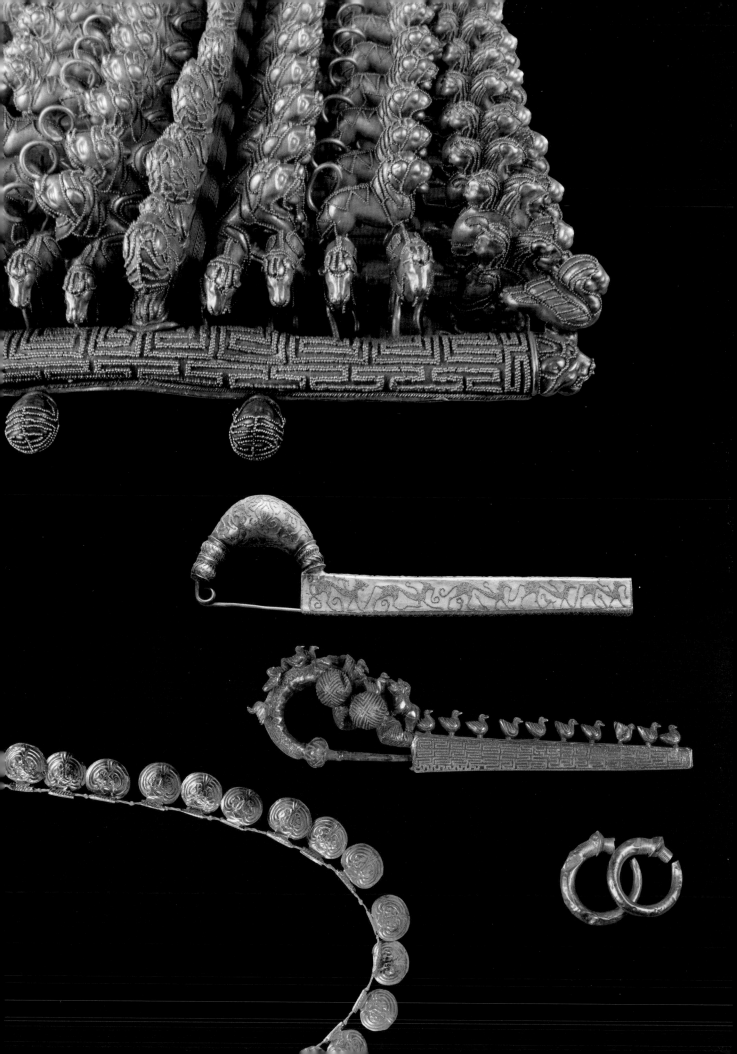

THE SIENESE VALDICHIANA
AND THE VALLEY OF THE OMBRONE

On the border between Tuscany and Umbria, it was once traversed by a river called the Clanis, a tributary of the Tiber that fed a catchment basin rich in water. All that survives today are the small lakes of Chiusi and Montepulciano, but in the past the river provided an easy line of communication with Southern Etruria and Rome. The suitability of this area for farming favored early settlement on the hillsides, and it is still possible to see the marks that this has left on the landscape.

A similar function of a link between cities on the coast (Vetulonia and Rusellae) and the inland parts of Northern Etruria was performed by the Ombrone River. The hilly areas that line its course, characterized by sparse vegetation in the fascinating region of the Crete but covered with dense scrub further to the south, still offer scenery of great beauty. More than anywhere else the presence of human beings appears discreet, almost marginal here, and the evocative power of the past maintains its fascination intact.

Chiusi

Opposite, detail of one of the facing slabs of the temple at I Fucoli, Chianciano, mid-2nd cent. BC. Museo Civico Archeologico delle Acque, Chianciano Terme

The entrance of a chamber tomb

Underground rooms in the necropolis of Poggio Gaiella

Evidence for the importance of the ancient city of Camars comes once again from its legendary origin, attributed by the sources to the mythical Clusius, son of Tyrrhenus the Lydian, or to Ulysses' son Telemachus. The hill to the west of the course of the Chiana River, where the Etruscans would build their city, appears to have been frequented in the Bronze Age, probably because of its strategic position. In the subsequent Iron Age (9th cent. BC), the territory of Chiusi saw the emergence of small settlements whose economy was purely at the subsistence level. One of these has been discovered at Montevenere. For this period only modest well tombs (Poggio Renzo, Fornace) are known, while the later Orientalizing necropolises brought to light on the hillsides around the town are signs of a marked increase in population and contain interments in jars, usually with individual depositions. At this time the city's "aristocratic" families buried their dead with lavish grave goods in monu-

mental chamber tombs carved out of the sandstone or built from blocks of stone, usually covered by mounds. Tombs of this type have been found at Poggio Gaiella. They have yielded large amounts of pottery imported from Corinth or Eastern Greece, and the remains of sculptures in fetid limestone representing fantastic animals with pieces of decorations that must have adorned an altar. The contents of the Pania Tomb were rich too and included an

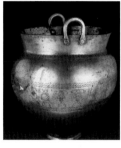

The silver-gilt *situla* of Plikasna with a detail of the upper band of decoration, from the Pania Tomb at Chiusi, mid-7th cent. BC. Museo Archeologico, Florence

Ivory box from the Pania Tomb at Chiusi, mid-7th cent. BC. Museo Archeologico, Florence

ivory box adorned with scenes from the Odyssey. In the closing decades of the 7th century the aristocratic class of Camars showed a preference for bronze ossuaries, sometimes set on thrones finely decorated with fantastic animals in repoussé.

The oldest remains connected with the city have been identified at Petriolo, a no longer urbanized area where recent excavations have identified a sort of artisans' district filled with potteries. In fact the economic and cultural fervor that characterized Camars over the course of the 6th century favored a lively local handicraft industry that specialized chiefly in

the production of richly decorated *bucchero* ware and objects in ivory, like the box from Poggio alla Sala or the so-called Palagi plates. At the same time it encouraged the importation of luxury objects from Greece (such as the extraordinary *François Vase*) or Southern Etruria, of which the city became a "center of distribution" for the inland areas of Etruria.

Toward the end of the 6th cent. BC the history of Chiusi was bound up with its king Porsenna, an influential figure who must have dominated the league of twelve Etruscan peoples, and in an attempt to restore Tarquinius Superbus to the throne even conquered Rome for a short time. At this moment the city attained the peak of its power and a high level of prosperity based on the cultivation of cereals, vines and olives in the fertile countryside, a practice that the literary sources tell us continued in later periods.

This affluence is also reflected in a number of tombs with wall paintings dating from the first half of the 5th century, of which only the ones in the tombs of the Monkey (480 BC) and the Hill (470 BC) have been preserved. On the walls of the former, cross-shaped with four chambers, we see the figure of the deceased, a woman, sheltered by a parasol and ringed by musicians and athletes performing in her honor. The tomb gets its name from the image of a

Two images of the
frescoes of the tomb
of the Hill, 470 BC.

little monkey tied to a tree in the central chamber. The second is entered through a stone door with two leaves that still open and close and has scenes of diners, chariot races and athletic contests on the walls.

While the painted tombs should be connected with the presence of craftsmen from Tarquinii, in this period the local artisans specialized in the production of *cippi* in fetid limestone, with carved scenes closely resembling the ones painted in the tombs.

At the beginning of the 4th century the city was besieged by the Gauls, drawn according to the sources by the rich products of the surrounding countryside. Leaving aside their romanticized treatment of the story, these accounts hint at the scale of the trade that went on between the fertile Valdichiana and the northern part of Italy. The city's aristocrats remained wealthy into the 3rd cent. BC, as is apparent from the Tomb of the Female Pilgrim (open to the public) where several generations of the Sentinate family were buried. The alabaster urns and the sarcophagi that can still be seen inside the tomb, just as its discoverers found them, are examples of a typical local production that was expanded in the early decades of the 2nd century to materials like travertine and terracotta.

This century saw a marked increase in population and the landscape was dotted with settlements of an agricultural character, perhaps a consequence of the emancipation and subsequent integration of large numbers of slaves who had taken part in the rebellions of 196 BC. The city seems to have been ruled by a few noble families of ancient lineage, while the much more numerous middle and upper classes displayed a high degree of literacy. From this period date the tombs of Vigna Grande and the Grand Duke, constructed from blocks of travertine, and a small painted tomb discovered at the locality of Tassinaia. An area devoted to the production of pottery has also been brought to light at Marcianella.

The participation of Clusium, as the Romans called the city, in the civil war led to its destruction and the confiscation of large swathes of territory to be granted to Sulla's veterans. From this time on the agrarian landscape underwent significant changes with the establishment of large villas worked by slaves.

Chianciano

The oldest vestiges uncovered in the area of Chianciano provide evidence of a remarkable flowering in the Orientalizing period, as is apparent from the large necropolis of Tolle, still under excavation, where several hundred 7th-century tombs have been found so far. Particularly common are Canopic vases (ossuaries with anthropomorphic features characteristic of the Chiusi area) deposited in jars, box and chamber tombs, along with large amounts of locally made and imported pottery. The landowning aristocracy paraded its status in the "princely" tomb of the Morelli Necropolis, with its exceptional set of bronzes from the end of the 7th century. More in general, however, the finds that have been made demonstrate the great vitality of this region in the Archaic period too.

Already famous in antiquity for its numerous mineral springs, Chianciano was the seat, in the Etruscan era, of important sanctuaries linked to the cult of water. In addition to the remains of a place of worship dedicated first to Apollo and then to Diana, extraordinary fragments of a bronze offering to the gods with statues of men (5th cent. BC) and women on a chariot (4th cent. BC) have been found at the locality of Sillene. At another sanctuary lo-

Lid of cinerary urn representing the deceased and Vanth, second half of the 5th cent. BC, and Mater Matuta, circa 470 BC., from the Pedata Necropolis at Chianciano. Museo Archeologico, Florence

cated at I Fucoli, and associated with a divine savior, has been uncovered part of a terracotta pediment (2nd cent. BC) with exquisitely molded statues that are now on display at the local Museo Civico Archeologico. At the nearby locality of Poggio Bacherina can be seen the remains of a farm with rooms used for making wine, destroyed in the early decades of the 1st cent. BC.

Particularly rich tombs, now partly open to the public, have been found in the Pedata Necropolis, from where come the famous cinerary statues of fetid limestone representing, respectively, a woman holding a child (the so-called Mater Matuta) and a dead man accompanied by the winged god Vanth, displaying the scroll of destiny. Impressive ruins of the luxurious baths that were built here in the Roman era can be seen at Mezzomiglio and Le Camerelle.

Sarteano

Reconstruction of the tomb with Canopic jars in the Macchiapiana Necropolis, Sarteano, late 7th-early 6th cent. BC. Museo Civico Archeologico, Sarteano

The site of important vestiges from prehistoric times, Sarteano is also known for its vast necropolises reflecting a great flowering in the Orientalizing period. These burial grounds, which extend along the hillsides of Solaia, Poggio Rotondo and Macchiapiana, must have been located close to scattered settlements that depended on the agricultural resources of the region and on stock rearing. The considerable affluence of the local aristocracy is apparent from the discovery of numerous Canopic vases in jar and chamber tombs, some of them housing double interments, with substantial grave goods that occasionally include pottery imported from Greece.

The huge necropolis of the Palazzina contains a tomb with the remains of a wall painting from the end of the 6th century, representing the deceased being conducted to the other world. Finds of considerable value from later centuries have also been made and for the most part can be seen at the local Museo Civico Archeologico. They reflect a high degree of prosperity: an exceptional example of this is the recent discovery at the locality of Pianacce (site of an extensive and rich necropolis that is open to the public) of a second painted tomb from the final decades of the 4th cent. BC, called the tomb of the "Infernal Quadriga." In it is depicted the striking figure of a demon with red hair, quite unlike other representations of this kind.

The graves of the Hellenistic period continue to bear witness to the vitality of the region of Sarteano, with their sarcophagi made of alabaster and travertine and numerous urns of high quality, such as the ones found in the tomb of the Cumere family, while the funerary architecture is extremely varied, with *dromoi* sometimes of great length used to house a large number of burials in small niches in the walls. An interesting example of this can be seen at the burial complex excavated at Mulin Canale.

In the Roman era the beauty of the landscape and the plentiful supply of water led to the construction of imposing villas decorated with figurative slabs and mosaics. Significant remains of these can be seen at the locality of Peschiera.

Alabaster cinerary urn from the tomb of the Cumere family, Sarteano, first half of the 3rd cent. BC. Museo Archeologico Nazionale, Siena

Face of the demon Charun in the tomb of the Infernal Quadriga in the Pianacce Necropolis, Sarteano, last decades of the 4th cent. BC

pp. 144-5: two faces of the cippus in fetid limestone from Sant'Angelo, Sarteano, last decades of the 6th cent. BC. Museo Civico Archeologico, Sarteano

Murlo

In Etruscan times the hill of Poggio Civitate, bounded to the west by the course of the Creole, a tributary of the Ombrone River, was the location of an important aristocratic residence. And in the nearby area significantly known as Piano del Tesoro, or "Plain of the Treasure," held by popular tradition to be the site of fabulous riches, a princely abode dating from the 7th cent. BC has been identified and brought to light. Perhaps destroyed by fire, the large building with a quadrangular plan was reconstructed in the 6th century. At the center lay a large uncovered area surrounded by a wooden colonnade, onto which opened numerous rooms used for household activities. The architectural decoration (reassembled in the local museum) set on top of the roof consisted of seated male figures wearing large hats, identified as images of the family's ancestors, alternating with sphinxes. The base of the walls was built of stone and the upper part of unfired

Acroterion with horseman, last three decades of the 7th cent. BC; acroterial statue of a man, early decades of the 6th cent. BC, from the princely palace at Murlo. Antiquarium di Poggio Civitate, Murlo

Reconstruction of a section of the roof of the princely palace at Murlo, early decades of the 6th cent. BC. Antiquarium di Poggio Civitate, Murlo

Facing slab with scene of assembly, early decades of the 6th cent. BC; bucchero *kyathos*, last three decades of the 7th cent. BC, from the princely palace at Murlo. Antiquarium di Poggio Civitate, Murlo

clay spread over an internal framework of branches and reeds. The excavations have shown that the settlement was abandoned deliberately around 525 BC, when the ornamental terracottas were buried in pits dug for the purpose. From then on the site was no longer occupied on a permanent basis.

Another large building has been uncovered at the southern end of the plateau and identified as a workshop used for the production of pottery, decorative slabs and small objects in bronze, ivory, horn and bone. Other parts of the same building must have been used for the processing of foodstuffs. Rich graves connect-

ed with the residence at Murlo have been found at Poggio Aguzzo, where excavations on the western side of the hill have brought to light pit tombs containing finely decorated *impasto* and *bucchero* ware.

Asciano

The Etruscan settlement in the area of Asciano, whose exact location is unknown, went through a period of great prosperity between the 7th and 6th cent. BC, as the finds made at the tumulus of the Mulinello have recently revealed. The importance of this center derived from the presence of an aristocratic class whose wealth came from farming and from exploitation of the travertine quarries, which appear to have been worked since as far back as the end of the 7th cent. BC.

The fortunate position in the valley of the Ombrone, which permitted easy communica-

tions with Vetulonia and Rusellae, must have favored the development of the settlement in the vicinity of Asciano. The imported painted vases of Greek and Etruscan manufacture found in the tombs excavated at Poggio Pinci, dating from between the 5th and the 1st cent. BC, testify to the continuing vitality of this area, and the existence of important families connected with the landed aristocracy is documented by tombs like the large one of the Hepni, in which around thirty people were buried, the last of them in the Augustan age. (G.P.)

The Cult of Water

Etruria is particularly rich in springs and for centuries its inhabitants have set great store by the curative qualities of their waters. The veneration of springs for their therapeutic properties was almost always presided over by Apollo and Hercules, although they were associated with other divinities as well: Silvanus, Asclepius and the Nymphs, lovers of hot or cold springs. The clear waters that flowed from them were believed to be capable of restoring people to health. Devotees expressed their gratitude to the deity with libations or an offering that represented the part of the body that had been cured: the deposits of such objects found in sacred areas discovered in the vicinity of curative springs commonly contain human heads and statuettes made of clay or bronze, anatomical ex-votos, crockery and coins. If animals were healed by the therapeutic properties attributed to the waters, zoomorphic figures in terracotta or bronze were offered to the guardian deity.

Many of the rural springs must have been left in their natural state and the only record of their use survives in the votive deposits uncovered nearby, but in some cases modest structures were erected for the worship of salutary divinities who had become the objects of an ingenuous and popular faith. At a number of springs more extensive places of worship were constructed in the immediate vicinity. In some cases, such as the Sillene and Fucoli springs at Chianciano Terme, the 5th-century sanctuaries were particularly imposing, with rich collections of votive offerings in bronze. In the successive Hellenistic and Roman eras many sources were enclosed by luxurious *thermae* of monumental appearance and the people who used them had to visit the sanctuary attached to the spring before entering the bath structures.

The power of a divine being over waters could also be manifested in springs located inside natural caves, where the rituals carried out were linked exclusively to the sphere of maternity. Meteoric water had its own specific deities, as did seawater, of which evidence survives at the sanctuary of Leucothea at Pyrgi. Large rivers like the Tiber and the Arno certainly had their own gods, but so did some minor ones like the Chiana, whose memory is preserved by the inscription on a small bronze figure of an athlete. Forms of veneration also took place on the shores of the great lakes of Central Italy and in the vicinity of smaller bodies of water located in the solitude of the mountains, like the one on Monte Falterona, linked to the nearby springs of the Arno. Along with large quantities of splendid statuettes in bronze, arrows have been found here that may well have been shot into the water from the land, perhaps for propitiatory reasons or as a symbolic act in which the arrow was identified with a divine thunderbolt. (G.P.)

Acroterion with female genius from the temple at I Fucoli, Chianciano, mid-2nd cent. BC. Museo Civico Archeologico delle Acque, Chianciano Terme

The Museo Archeologico Nazionale in Chiusi

I The museum in Chiusi was opened in 1871, displaying materials donated by the local aristocracy and clergy. The collections were transferred to their present location, built for the purpose, in 1901, and include finds made in excavations conducted in the area around Chiusi, arranged according to chronological criteria. The oldest exhibits date from the Bronze Age (11th-10th cent. BC), with objects from Poggio Gaiella and the Parco dei Forti that indicate the presence of settlements of huts where the carving of deer horn and weaving were practiced. The objects documenting the Iron Age (9th-8th cent. BC) also come from villages discovered in various localities of the region, including Montevenere, where a large quantity of earthenware has been brought to light. Grave goods from well tombs excavated at Poggio Renzo in 1872 can be dated to the same period. In addition to biconical ossuaries, there is a lid with two figures embracing on top, representing the leave-taking from this world. The later Orientalizing period (7th-6th cent. BC) is documented by *impasto* pottery and bronze objects that bear witness to the already thriving trade between Chiusi, coastal Etruria and the Faliscan area. Also on display are the rich contents of the tomb of the Pania, made famous by an ivory *box* —

its place taken here by a copy – with scenes drawn from the myth of Odysseus.

The collection of *buccheri* comprises examples decorated with narrow bands of human figures, produced by rolling the soft clay with a cylinder incised with a recessed design, and later examples with lavish stamped decorations. The section also contains a group of Canopic jars, cinerary urns peculiar to this area whose anthropomorphic characteristics were believed to make the body whole again following its destruction in the rite of cremation. One of the most interesting Canopic jars on show is the one known as Dolciano (after the name

Lid of cinerary urn from Poggio Renzo, Chiusi, 8th cent. BC.

Stone sphinx from Chiusi, first half of the 6th cent. BC.

Bucchero krater from Chiusi, mid-6th cent. BC.

Opposite, the Canopic jar
of Dolciano, last decades
of the 7th cent. BC.

The "Paolozzi Ossuary"
from Dolciano, near Chiusi,
620 BC.

Cinerary urn with roof-shaped lid, from Chiusi, first half of the 5th cent. BC

Terracotta cinerary urn with figure of craftsman on the lid, from Chiusi, 2nd cent. BC

Small terracotta urns representing Charon with the deceased and the gate of Hades, from Chiusi, 2nd cent. BC

Two faces of the *skyphos* with scenes from the *Odyssey* attributed to the Painter of Penelope, mid-5th cent. BC

Reconstruction of the Tassinaie Tomb, 170-150 BC

of the place it was found): dating from the closing decades of the 7th century, it has a bronze throne and ossuary and a clay head. The *Paolozzi Ossuary* with a female figure on the lid can be assigned to the same period. The sculptures carved from *pietra fetida*, a kind of sandstone rich in sulfur that was given this name by 19th-century excavators because of the unpleasant smell it gives off when scratched, are also linked to the funerary sphere. They include monuments on a demanding scale like the stepped one from the necropolis of Poggio Gaiella, memorial stones, sometimes in the form of a house, cinerary urns and sarcophagi carved in very low relief with scenes of banqueting, games and sacrifices in honor of the deceased. Another type of funerary sculpture is that of the real and fantastic figures which were set up to guard tombs by their apotropaic powers, i.e. their ability to drive away evil influences. The display continues with figured pottery of Attic and Etruscan manufacture, including a red-figure *skyphos* with scenes from the *Odyssey*: Telemachus and Penelope at the loom and the recognition of Ulysses by his nurse Eurycleia. From the later Hellenistic era (3rd-2nd cent. BC) come numerous terracotta cinerary urns stamped with designs on the front and the small tomb of the Tassinaie with a

painted decoration of festoons and images of the deceased. Among the Roman materials in the museum are a large number of sculptures found within the city limits, such as the *Portrait of Augustus* and the remains of mosaic floors. A particularly fine example of the latter depicts a wild boar and stag hunt. The display concludes with materials from the Longobard period uncovered in the necropolis of Arcisa. (G.P.)

Urn of Larth Sentinates Caesa from the tomb of the Female Pilgrim at Chiusi, early 3rd cent. BC

EASTERN ETRURIA

Opposite, a detail of
the bronze chandelier
from Fratta, Cortona,
4th cent. BC.
Museo dell'Accademia
Etrusca, Cortona

The Valdichiana
in the direction of Lake
Trasimeno

In antiquity the eastern part of Etruria was characterized by the convergence of three valleys, those of the Arno, Tiber and Clanis. What remains of the latter is now called the Chiana, but before the reclamation initiated at the time of grand-ducal Tuscany it was a river that flowed into the Tiber through the Paglia. On the other side of the broad basin of Lake Trasimeno stood Perugia, a short distance from the Tiber, which had always formed the natural boundary between the Etruscans and the other populations of Italy. The lines of communication along the river valleys also linked Southern Etruria, and thus the cities on the coast as well, with Northern Etruria and Aemilia. In fact Cortona and Arezzo are located on one of these routes, and so is Castiglion Fiorentino, which was a junction on not just the north-south axis but the east-west one as well, i.e. the route between the Adriatic coast and the Valtiberina.

The fertile territory was dotted with Etruscan settlements and rural sanctuaries, extending as far as the Casentino and the source of the Arno, where many votive offerings of Etruscan, Umbrian and Greek manufacture have been found in the area of an ancient lake, dubbed the "lake of the idols" as a result.

The "Falterona Warrior,"
420-400 BC.
British Museum, London

Cortona

The ancient settlement occupied the same site as the medieval and Renaissance city, on a spur of Monte Sant'Egidio overlooking the fertile Valdichiana and about 10 km from the northern shore of Lake Trasimeno. The origins of Cortona are not very clear, but in the customary legends its foundation is attributed to the Pelasgians, or to Corito the son of Dardanus, mythical ancestor of Aeneas.

There is little mention of the city in the literary sources apart from a reference to its defeat, along with Arezzo and Perugia, by the Romans (310 BC), after which it succeeded in obtaining a truce that lasted for 30 years. Cortona's name appeared again in relation to the battle at Lake Trasimeno between Hannibal and the Romans (217 BC), but it did not figure in the list of Etruscan cities that promised

**Two views
of the podium-altar
of the mound known as
"Melone II del Sodo,"
580-560 BC**

assistance for Scipio's expedition against Carthage.

The city's great flowering in the Orientalizing period (7th cent. BC) is amply documented by the large burial mounds (known locally as *meloni* or "melons") visible at the foot of the hill on which it stands. The large one called

The tomb called "Tanella di Pitagora," 2nd cent. BC

Cinerary urn from Tomb A of the tumulus of Camucia near Cortona, late 7th cent. BC. Museo della Città Etrusca e Romana, Cortona

the "Melone II del Sodo" is spectacular: here two chamber tombs were discovered at different times, both of them unfortunately looted. The first has a long *dromos* with two vestibules in sequence leading to seven cells, six at the sides and one at the end. The other, quadrangular tomb, from a later date, housed inhumations in stone sarcophagi and cinerary urns. All that is left of the rich grave goods is a set of jewelry that somehow escaped the notice of the robbers. The importance of this mound stems essentially from the presence of a large "altar-terrace": one of a kind, it has a flight of steps leading to a platform originally covered by a roof of wood and brick decorated with figured slabs. The extraordinary parapet has double volutes with sculptural elements at the base representing a warrior locked in combat with a wild beast.

The bronze chandelier from Fratta, Cortona, 4th cent. BC. Museo dell'Accademia Etrusca, Cortona

"Slab of the Mourners," stone funeral bed from Tomb A of the tumulus of Camucia near Cortona, second half of the 6th cent. BC. Museo della Città Etrusca e Romana, Cortona

About 300 m away stands the other sepulchral monument known as the "Melone I del Sodo," containing a large aristocratic tomb that was used for several generations to judge by the inscription in Etruscan carved on a lintel of much more recent date. In it mention is made of a member of the Mefana family, probably of Umbrian origin. The "Melone di Camucìa," also divided into two large tombs with several chambers, belonged to another "prince." The sumptuous grave goods included a bronze ossuary, numerous vases and a funeral bed with female figures kneeling in mourning carved on the front. The other tombs uncovered a short distance from the city are from a later date (2nd cent. BC) and consist of mortuary chambers built out of blocks of stone and covered with tunnel vaults, known locally as the "Tanella di Pitagora" and "Tanella Angori"; all that remains of the latter is the base.

Substantial sections of the ancient city's walls, constructed out of large blocks of "millstone" grit, have survived, along with a few remains of buildings. From what may have been a sanctuary at the nearby locality of Fratta comes the celebrated bronze chandelier (4th cent. BC) now in the local Museo dell'Accademia Etrusca. It has a complex ornamentation with figures of harpies alternating with satyrs and a large, beautifully crafted Gorgon's head at the center. A much more recent discovery is the so-called *Tabula cortonensis* (late 3rd-early 2nd cent. BC), a bronze panel with a long inscription in Etruscan relating to a land transaction near Cortona.

Above, small bronze of Tinia
with thunderbolt from
Firenzuola, 5th cent. BC;
above, small bronze of winged
deity, 6th cent. BC. Museo
dell'Accademia Etrusca, Cortona

Two-faced statuette of Culsans
with inscription, from the
sanctuary of Porta Bifora at
Cortona, first half of the
3rd cent. BC. Museo
dell'Accademia Etrusca, Cortona

Castiglion Fiorentino

Substantial remains of an Etruscan settlement of the Archaic period that probably had the function of exercising control over the valley of the Clanis below have recently been identified inside the majestic keep of Castiglion Fiorentino, between Cortona and Arezzo. The archeological data shows that the site was already frequented in prehistoric times, but it is not until the late Archaic era that the evidence grows more significant and documents the existence of a sanctuary, adorned with slabs painted with Gorgon's heads, dating from the late 5th-early 4th cent. BC. The place of worship was still in use in the 2nd cent. BC, the date of the potsherds and several slabs with floral motifs in relief that have been found there.

In the Hellenistic period the small town was surrounded with massive defensive walls.

Arezzo

Located on a low hill at the place where the fertile and level Valdichiana meets the hilly and wild Casentino, the city owes its origin to its favorable geographic position, at an obligatory point of passage on the routes to Emilia Romagna and the Po Valley in the north and the Valtiberina in the east.

Faint traces of a ring of walls of uncertain date show that the ancient city stood in the area now comprised between the Medici Fortress and the cathedral. Its economy must have been based on agricultural exploitation of the plain below, and the settlement was probably founded in the second half of the 6th cent. BC, judging by the box and pit tombs with figured pottery, bronzes and jewelry found in the necropolis of Poggio al Sole. The deposit of votive offerings at Fonte Veneziana containing bronze statuettes of *kouroi* and *korai* was formed in the same period. Figurative terracotta slabs of high quality, demonstrating the existence of an established school of crafts-

Small votive bronzes from Arezzo, 7th and 6th cent. BC. Museo Archeologico Nazionale, Arezzo

Opposite, the "Chimera of Arezzo," 400-350 BC. Museo Archeologico, Florence

manship, come from Piazza San Jacopo, seat of a sanctuary in the 5th century, and a large collection of ex-votos has been uncovered near the bastion of Porta San Lorentino. From this area also comes the celebrated sculpture of the *Chimera*, a masterpiece of 4th-century Etruscan bronze work discovered in the middle of the 16th century during the construction of the city walls.

The literary sources tell us that in the 4th century Arezzo was riven by strong social tensions stemming from the aspiration of the lower classes, chiefly employed in the local pottery and metal workshops, to play a part in the government of the city, in the hands of a small group of aristocrats. These tensions culminated in the outbreak of true revolts, the first of which was put down by the intervention of Aule Spurinna of Tarquinii (358 BC), while the second, against the wealthy family of the Cilnii, was suppressed by Roman troops (302 BC).

The military pressure exerted on the cities of Etruria by the Romans at the beginning of the 3rd century was brought to bear on Arezzo too, and the city was forced to pay a very heavy tribute to obtain peace. Yet this did not result in economic decline. At the turn of the century, on the contrary, it was still a flourishing center capable of making a major contribution to Scipio's expedition against Carthage. Over

Sections of the first city walls built of stone, 5th cent. BC

View of the amphitheater, 1st cent. AD

the following decades the city continued to thrive, notwithstanding the slave rebellions that disrupted Northern Etruria between 196 and 186 BC, and this was largely due to the privileged relations that it had established with Rome. Testimony to this is provided by the rich terracotta decorations from the temples at Catona and Santacroce, as well as the particularly large deposit of votive offerings found on Via della Società Operaia. The sanctuary of Castelsecco, visible on the hill of San Cornelio 3 km from the city, evidently also dates from a period of renewed construction. It was linked with a theater with its own scene building, decorated with terracotta slabs, where the Etruscan tragedies mentioned by the Latin writer Varro were staged, perhaps along with those of the Greek tradition.

Arezzo's involvement in the civil war, when it sided with Mario like the other Etruscan cities, led to repression by Sulla and the founding of a colony of veterans who were known as *Arretini fidentiores*.

Arezzo maintained its reputation as a center for the production of black-glazed pottery throughout the 2nd century and the following one, but toward the end of the 1st the city became known for its fine tableware, plain or decorated in relief and finished with a brilliant coral glaze. It was made in a large number of potteries that stamped their products (from AD 15 onward) with a trademark in the form of a small human foot bearing the manufacturer's name. This extensive production, which spread rapidly all over the Roman empire and should be seen in relation to a substantial expansion in the size of the city in the Augustan age, may well have been linked with the figure of Maecenas. A noble citizen of Arezzo and descendant of the aristocratic Cilnii family, he became the friend and counselor of Augustus, who referred to him, together with his city and its excellent ceramics, in a letter cited by Seneca.

From Roman Arretium, still flourishing in the 1st cent. AD, survive the imposing remains of an amphitheater that could hold up to 8000 spectators.

Pieve a Socana

The parish church of Sant'Antonino with, in the foreground, remains of the Etruscan sanctuary of the 5th cent. BC

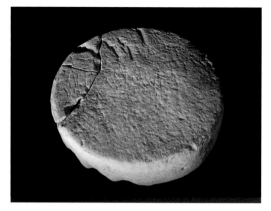

Large stone disk with dedication to the sun from the Etruscan sanctuary of Pieve a Socana, 5th cent. BC. Museo Archeologico Nazionale, Arezzo

Remains of an Etruscan sanctuary have been brought to light at the medieval church of Sant'Antonino at Pieve a Socana, bearing witness to the continuity of worship at this sacred place. A large sacrificial altar and a flight of steps have been identified as belonging to the ancient sanctuary, which had the opposite orientation to the Christian church. The building was adorned with terracottas datable to the 5th cent. BC, and some small altars and large stone disks with dedications to the Sun come from the same period. The presence of a number of terracotta antefixes indicate that it was redecorated in the 2nd cent. BC. The sanctuary must have served the religious needs of the rural population and travelers on the important road along the right bank of the Arno to Mount Falterona. The loss of this route's importance brought about a rapid decline of the sanctuary, which was abandoned at the beginning of the 1st cent. BC.

Perugia

Bowl attributed to the "Group of the Little Masters," from Tomb 19 of the necropolis of the Palazzone at Perugia, second half of the 6th cent. BC. Museo Archeologico, Perugia

The literary sources offer a plethora of theories about the origin of Perugia, which is ascribed to the Umbrian tribe of the Sarsinates, to Achaean veterans of the Trojan War or to Aulestes, who was the father or brother of Ocnus, the mythical founder of Bologna and Mantua; a hypothesis, this last, that appears to allude to the role played by the cities of Northern Etruria in the Etruscan colonization of the Po Valley. Evidence for the antiquity of the settlement at Perugia comes in any case from finds from the Iron Age made in the necropolis of the Palazzone.

Its strategic position at the junction of the lines of communication between the upper valley of the Tiber and the Umbrian Valley contributed to the growth of the city, which was able to extend its influence over a vast swathe of territory exploited for agricultural purposes, and the cultivation of cereals in particular. According to Livy, Perugia had a particularly prestigious role in the Etruscan League toward the end of the 4th century and, along with

Detail of the Gate of Mars, second half of the 3rd cent. BC

Amphora from Tomb 172 of the necropolis of the Palazzone at Perugia. Museo Archeologico, Perugia

sections of paved road and parts of buildings belonging to the Roman city have come to light.

Better known are the cemeteries that have yielded evidence from as far back as the Iron Age, in particular the huge necropolis of the Palazzone, where rich graves with Attic pottery and *bucchero* ware have been found, It also contains the monumental hypogeum of the Velimna-Volumni family with burials dating

Volsinii, supplied a large military contingent during the clashes with the Romans of those years. The defeat at the battle of Sentinum in 295 BC led to the exaction of a very high tribute from Perugia, as from the other inland cities of Northern Etruria. After 90 BC it became a Roman *municipium* and was assigned to the Tromentina tribe. A half century later, after giving refuge to Mark Antony's brother, Lucius, it was besieged by Octavian Augustus, taken by storm and burned (40 BC). It was then reconstructed and given the name of Augusta Perusia.

Owing to the continuity of life in the medieval and modern eras, part of the ancient city's ring of walls has been preserved: built of blocks of travertine, it stretched for about 3 km and had monumental gates. Two of them have survived, both from the second half of the 3rd cent. BC: the Gate of Mars, incorporated into the Rocca Paolina and adorned with busts of Jupiter and the Dioscuri and horse's heads, and the Gate of Augustus, flanked by two Roman-built towers and with a round arch surmounted by a decoration of shields and pilasters. It is likely that the Sorbello Well (recently restored and opened to the public), with its facing of blocks of travertine, was related to the construction of the walls. At various times from between the 2nd and 1st cent. BC. The tomb, one of the most interesting of the late Etruscan era, consists of a central vestibule onto which open four cells and a corridor at the back leading to three more mortuary chambers. It offers a good example of the interior of a house from the Hellenistic period, with the vestibule covered by a pitched ceiling with realistic carvings of the wooden structure of the roof and a pediment at the rear adorned with an emblem in relief between two heads. The central chamber, decorated with a Gorgon's head on the ceiling, housed the oldest burials, in cinerary urns of remarkable refinement. That of the founder of the family, Arnth Velimnes, an important magistrate in 2nd-cent.-BC Perugia, is particularly sumptuous, with the figure of the deceased reclining on a lid

The interior of the hypogeum of the Volumni in the necropolis of the Palazzone, 2nd cent. BC

The two ends of the sarcophagus from the Sperandio necropolis, Perugia, early 5th cent. BC. Museo Archeologico, Perugia

supported by two winged demons (*lase*) standing guard at a painted door. Very rich too are the tombs excavated in the Sperandio Necropolis, from where comes the celebrated sarcophagus of fetid limestone (Museo Archeologico, Perugia) with a representation of a parade. Its significance has been interpreted in various ways: return from a military expedition, migration of clans to Perugia or departure of a leader for the Po Valley.

The monumental tomb of San Manno, with a tunnel vault constructed of blocks of travertine, belonged to the Precu family, as we are told by an inscription at the entrance of one of the lateral cells. The cross-shaped tomb of the Cai Cutu family, discovered still intact at the locality of Monteluce, has been reconstructed in the Archeological Museum. It contained 50 cinerary urns, some of very fine craftsmanship, and a sarcophagus, dating from a long period that stretched from the 3rd to the 1st cent. BC.

Todi

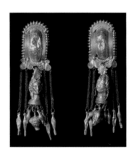

Gold earrings from the necropolis of the Peschiera at Todi, early 3rd cent. BC. Museo Nazionale Etrusco di Villa Giulia, Rome

Todi stands on an elevation between the Tiber and the small Naia and Rio rivers, in an ideal position to exercise control over the important watercourse and the road that led to Volsinii. The Etruscan name of this ancient Umbrian city, Tutere (*tute* = boundary), is a reference to its geographic location on the border, as the literary sources make clear. The city entered the Etruscan political sphere in the 5th century, when it experienced a period of great economic prosperity that was to last for two centuries and even prompted it to mint a coin of its own inscribed with the name Tuter. From this period date the graves in the necropolis of

the Peschiera containing large quantities of beautifully crafted bronze artifacts, jewelry and Greek and Etruscan figured pottery. The deposit of votive offerings in the suburban sanctuary of Monte Santo is datable to the 4th cent. BC, and it was here that the famous bronze statue known as the *Mars of Todi*, now in the Vatican Museums, was found. Todi's affluence is well documented up until the 3rd cent. BC, when it came under Roman rule. (G.P.)

Opposite, the Mars of Todi, early 4th cent. BC. Museo Gregoriano Etrusco, Vatican

The *Tabula Cortonensis* and Land Law

The bronze plate found in fragments at Cortona several years ago by a private citizen (who only provided very vague indications as to the site), constitutes a discovery of great importance to our understanding of language and law in Etruria. It is in fact one of the most important finds with an epigraphic content ever made since, with its 40 lines and 206 words, it is now the third longest text available to us in Etruscan, after the "Zagreb mummy wrapping," with a list of rituals written on cloth, and the "Capua tile," engraved with a calendar of festivals. The *Tabula* is a rectangular panel about 50 cm in height, broken into eight pieces, only seven of which have survived, and is covered with writing on the whole of one side and part of the other.

The object originally had two pivots, on which it evidently turned so that it could be read on both sides. Exposed to public view for a long time, as the thick patina that had formed on it before it was broken also shows, the *tabula* is inscribed with a text that is essentially a legal contract. Engraved by two different scribes in the 3rd-2nd cent. BC, it relates to the transfer of plots of land, including a vineyard, by sale or rent. The document gives the names of the contracting parties and numerous witnesses, as well as indications of clauses, customary practices and the public officials that controlled them, along with some interesting references to the places involved. Unfortunately not all of the text has been preserved: one of the pieces is missing and there are encrustations that make it difficult to read. However, attempts at translation have been made, one of which interprets it as a transaction between some landowners, the family of the Cusu, to which the main person mentioned in the deed (Petru Skevas) belonged, and a group of buyers. A public official – the *zilath mekl rasnal* – was one of the witnesses or "guarantors" of the transaction. Another slightly conflicting hypothesis construes the entire document as a contract between different families relating solely to lease of the land, drawn up in front of numerous witnesses.

Whatever the interpretation, the interest of the artifact lies in what it has to tell us about the history of land contracts. It is thought that documents of this kind must have been one the earliest applications of writing, introduced into Etruria at the end of the 8th cent. BC, since the continuity and protection of private landed property – something which, perhaps not coincidentally, became widespread in the same period – requires by definition lasting and impartial agreements. For millennia these have been guaranteed exclusively by written contracts. It is worth pointing out that, with deeds of land ownership, the measurement of land and the marking of plots with boundary stones must have become common in Etruria, presupposing the existence of sophisticated techniques of surveying. So, with the passing of the centuries and the increase in such transactions, it can be assumed that many deeds of this kind were drawn up, and yet the *Tabula* is the only one to have been found so far in Etruria. Such a grave gap, with its implications for our understanding of the Etruscan legal system, cannot be easily bridged.

Yet it is possible to deduce some characteristics of Etruscan land law from a reading of this text: in the Cortona plate, the lack of any reference to the duration of the contract suggests that it was valid "for life," or may even have been permanent and transferable. It should be remembered that – according to Latin literary sources – the prophetess Vegoia had declared that boundary stones marking the ownership of land in Etruria, protected by Jupiter-Tinia, were eternal in character. The permanence of the relations established with the contract of the *Tabula* is underlined by the involvement of descendants, in the guise of guarantors, suggesting that this was a characteristic of Etruscan law. In fact many of the people listed are accompanied by their children and grandchildren, indicating

The cippus of Perugia, 3rd-2nd cent. BC. Museo Archeologico, Perugia

Opposite, the *Tabula Cortonensis*, 3rd-2nd cent. BC. Museo della Città Etrusca e Romana, Cortona

that the guarantee was seen as something that would be passed down over time and last forever.

The reliability of the contract is also assured by a number of people cited in the epigraph, probably surveyors, who were responsible for checking the measurements made in order to prevent fraud. There was also provision for the drafting of four copies of the contract by an office or board called the *sparza sazle*. The text found in Cortona contains an exceptional allusion to the overall structure of the Etruscan legal system, in the words designating the "Tarchie discipline." Through Etruscan images of him, this figure has been identified with the mythical Tages of Latin literature, the divine child who emerged from the earth at Tarquinii and dictated the elements of the *Etrusca disciplina*, i.e. the foundations of the religious and legal precepts on which that culture was based.

This markedly religious aspect of Etruscan law is also evident in the text of the "Perugia boundary stone," which can be considered an arbitration ruling on a dispute over land boundaries, predial servitude, water use and the right of access to a tomb between the Perugian families of the Velthina and the Afuna. Here too human law appears to be inextricably bound up with divine law, and the oath involves a commitment before men and gods on the basis of "Etruscan law" (*tesna rasna*), explicitly cited on the stone. (M.M.)

VOLTERRA AND THE SURROUNDING REGION

Central and Western Tuscany, which descends from the hills around Volterra to the sea and includes the stretch of coast between Pisa and Populonia, is today an area of great scenic beauty, although very different from the past. While the interior is now a barren, almost lunar landscape, it was once rich in vegetation and woodland, while the coastline was much further inland and dotted with sand bars and brackish lagoons.

In this setting lived the oldest inhabitants of the area, occupying the modest heights behind Livorno and the middle and lower Val di Cecina in the Lower and Middle Paleolithic. The human communities of the Neolithic preferred the humid zones in the plains, better suited to agriculture and stock raising, or the uplands (including those further inland): some of the finds made in these areas are now on display in the Museo Civico Archeologico of Cecina. From the following Copper Age date a number of graves discovered in the environs of Volterra and Livorno, while an area used for the working of metal has been brought to light near San Vincenzo. Various discoveries from between the early and late stages of the Bronze Age continue to bear witness to the central role played by this region in the diffusion of metal artifacts in Etruria.

While the context of many of the finds from these times is unknown, the cases of the Medicean Fortress of Livorno and Collesalvetti, dating from the end of the Bronze Age, are very different. The first discovery is the result of recent excavations inside two underground chambers of the fortress in Livorno, which have identified the foundations of at least three huts. Much larger is the site of the Pratini dell'Argin Grosso, in the commune of Collesalvetti, where construction work has brought to light a settlement built on piles on reclaimed land (mid-11th cent. BC), as the site was once located on the shores of a brackish lagoon.

While the upper part of the dwellings has vanished entirely, evidence of domestic life has been preserved, including hearths and firedogs, spindle whorls and loom weights used in spinning and weaving and the remains of land and sea animals, bearing witness to the diet of their inhabitants. A number of blue and turquoise glass beads show they had contacts with distant places.

A view of the Balze at Volterra

Opposite, the Inghirami Tomb at Volterra, 2nd cent. BC., reconstructed in the garden of the Archeological Museum in Florence

The Origins of Volterra

At the beginning of the Iron Age the most densely populated area was Volterra, where cemeteries with well tombs from as early as the 9th cent. BC have been found. In the area of Le Ripaie, on the southern side of the city, there are some very ancient tombs, with biconical ossuaries typical of the Villanovan culture. More graves of the same type date from the 8th century and contain metal objects (spearheads, bracelets, clasps, razors, chains and pendants), testifying to a flourishing metalworking industry in the district. The cemetery was also used in the following century, with well tombs in which the grave goods and the remains of the deceased were placed in a jar; some of the burials were in small chests made of stone slabs that foreshadow the chamber tombs. Showing obvious similarities to those of the Florentine region, they must have been connected with a nearby settlement, perhaps that of Castello on the acropolis: traces of a floor, pilework and a small bronze suggest that a place of worship was built here as early as the end of the 7th century.

But the elevation on which Volterra stands was the site of other settlements in the Villanovan period, owing to the presence of natural terracing and a view that allowed the inhabitants to observe the valleys of the Cecina, Elsa and Era, while from Guerruccia, near the Balze, it was possible to see the lower valley of the Arno as far as Pisa, and the Apennines and Apuan Alps beyond. In fact various minor Villanovan communities emerged on the plateau in the 8th cent. BC: graves with interesting contents have been found between Guerruccia, Badia and Santa Chiara, on Monte Bradoni and at Poggio alle Croci.

The materials from these tombs, on display in the local Museo Guarnacci, reflect the unbroken continuity of the Villanovan cultural tradition between the 9th and 7th century, in similar fashion to the Florentine territory with which this area had close contacts: the reason for this stability is more likely to lie in the existence of an established sociopolitical model than in a lack of relations with the outside world.

The increasing density of the graves in the necropolises of Volterra during the last quarter of the 8th century shows that population growth had already resulted in overcrowding. From this moment on, numerous minor settlements sprang up in a radial pattern around the city over the course of a few decades, as a consequence of the flight of aristocratic families from the "mother city" into the outlying areas, previously only sparsely inhabited.

Reconstruction of Tomb Q1 of the Ripaie Necropolis at Volterra, second half of the 7th cent. BC. Museo Etrusco Guarnacci, Volterra

Ribbed jar from an Orientalizing tomb, second half of the 7th cent. BC. Museo Etrusco Guarnacci, Volterra

Vada

The ancient center of Vada, located on the coast just to the north of the mouth of the Cecina River, was already in existence in the 9th cent. BC. A hut village of the Early Iron Age has been discovered in the area of Vada Volaterrana (now the locality of San Gaetano), which was Volterra's port in the Roman era. Along with the remains of buildings, traces relating to the environment in which the settlement stood have been uncovered, showing that it was laid out around a pool of seawater similar to others where villages had grown up on the northern Tyrrhenian shoreline. Evidence for the presence of Etruscans at Vada over the following centuries is provided by other finds and traces of settlement. In the Roman era the port of Va-

da Volaterrana acquired an importance that it would maintain until the turn of the 6th cent. AD and that is testified on the ground by the remains of the "Large Baths" and by the "Small Baths, *horrea* (warehouses), what was probably a *macellum*, a *schola* (seat of an association) and a monumental fountain, buildings which can now be visited in the Archeological Area of San Gaetano di Vada.

The materials from the port district are on display in the Museo Civico Archeologico of Rosignano Marittimo, along with prehistoric and protohistoric finds, the contents of Etruscan-Hellenistic tombs at Castiglioncello and tombs at Pian dei Lupi and objects that have been recovered from the seabed.

The Territory of Volterra and Casale Marittimo

The cinerary urn of Montescudaio with banqueting scene, mid-7th cent. BC. Museo Archeologico, Cecina

The interior of the southern tomb of the Montecalvario Tumulus at Castellina in Chianti, 7th cent. BC

The vast inland territory of Volterra, already inhabited in the Early Iron Age, also underwent changes between the 8th and 7th cent. BC. At some of the centers that dominated communications with the hinterland of Etruria or the passes through the Apennines have been found tumuli (e.g. that of Montecalvario at Castellina in Chianti), or necropolises, such as the Casone di Monteriggioni, which grew in size and wealth toward the 7th century. In fact chamber tombs containing large numbers of precious objects in *bucchero* and metal, as well as products that show an Oriental influence, date from this period.

On the western side of the Volterran region groups of tombs bear witness to the existence of settlements from the end of the 8th century onward, at Pomarance, Cerreta, Totolla and Guardistallo; from Montescudaio comes the celebrated *impasto* cinerary urn from the first half of the 7th cent. BC that is now in the Museo Archeologico of Cecina. It is a biconical vase of Villanovan tradition decorated with swastikas in relief, on whose handle is set a

Bronze shield, three-legged metal table and ax from Tomb A at Casale Marittimo, 8th-7th cent. BC. Museo Archeologico, Cecina

mourning human figure; the domed lid is decorated with a banqueting scene, in which a personage of high rank – undoubtedly the dead man – is seated on a stool at a three-legged table covered with food, perhaps served by the female figure next to him. On the other side of the table are set two kraters for wine. A testimony to the symbolic value of the banquet as a mark of prosperity, this object documents the traditional custom of eating while seated; it was not until the 6th century that the "Greek" style of dining while lying on a *kline* was introduced.

But the most exceptional archeological discoveries have been made at Casale Marittimo, where the necropolis of Casa Nocera has been identified, with tombs dating from between the end of the 8th and the beginning of the 6th cent. BC. Their contents are on display in the rooms of Cecina's Archeological Museum.

Tomb A of the cemetery, consisting of a

simple square chest of stone slabs, contained a *dolium* covered with a shield made of bronze plate. The bronze cinerary urn, on the other hand, was covered by a silver bowl and held the bones of the deceased wrapped up with his personal ornaments (a custom mentioned in Homeric poetry) in a linen cloth. Other luxury objects accompanied the remains of the head of this *gens*, among them a three-legged table, a dinner service with bronze cups, some of them produced in the East, and a vessel that still contained a honeycomb. In fact the excavation even yielded the remains of the ritual meal of the deceased, including grapes, apples, hazelnuts, pomegranates and resinated wine.

In the same necropolis at Casale Marittimo there was a pit with two separate but perhaps contemporary tombs of men: in addition to an incense burner, silver cup and gold, silver and

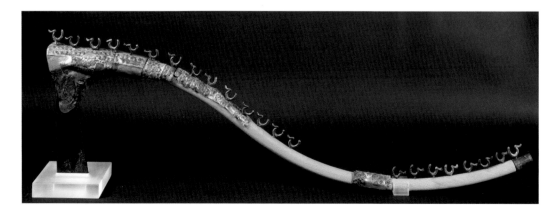

Funerary sculptures from the necropolis at Casale Marittimo, mid-7th cent. BC. Museo Archeologico, Cecina

bronze pins, the richer of the two contained an extremely unusual group of three bronze axes. The fact that these weapons were bound together in a "bundle" by a ring that passed through the handles of all three has led to the hypothesis that they were a symbol of authority. It is of considerable significance that the other, nearby grave also held more conventional weapons (a knife and a spear) and two axes linked together by a ring of bronze wire. Among the other graves was the tomb of a young warrior whose long braid of hair was garlanded with flowers; as well as arms and ornaments, the grave contained a bowl wrapped in linen cloth holding a ritual meal of hazelnuts, grapes and a pomegranate. Two limestone statues of young men dressed in oval belts and loincloths must once have stood on top of the small chamber tomb. Dated to the middle of the 7th cent. BC, they are the oldest full-relief sculptures of large size found in Etruria.

Volterra from the Archaic Period to Romanization

A stretch of Etruscan walls at Santa Chiara

While it was in the 7th cent. BC that the separate settlements in the Volterra area fused to form a city, not until the 6th is there any clear evidence of well-organized urban structures, such as the residential areas of Piano di Castello. It was here that the oldest buildings stood, protected by the first, short ring of walls around the acropolis, stretching for about 1300 m and dating from the same period. The chamber tombs carved out of the tufa at Guerruccia, Santa Chiara and San Giusto imitated the dwellings of this time and contained valuable goods imported from the Orient. In the first half of the 5th century a second ring of walls was erected, this time about 2 km long in order to encircle the 10 hectares of the urban area; houses as well as places of worship stood on the acropolis, and *bucchero* ware and Attic

red-figure pottery have often been found in the structures of the former. These imports from Attica are evidence for the importance of the coastal ports, and thus Vada as well as Populonia, through which direct trade with the Northern Tyrrhenian Sea and the Greek port of Massalia (Marseilles) presumably passed. The money in the treasure trove of Porta Penera, which comprised silver currency from Massalia and Phocaea as well as local coins, seems to be connected with these markets. The trade was fed not just by agriculture but also by the mining industry, which exploited the abundant copper present in surface veins in the Val di Cecina, between the Era and the Evola and at Montaione. The economic growth of Volterra also encouraged urban migration, and had repercussions on the social organization of the city's population.

While the structures on the acropolis underwent renovation, with the addition of cisterns, the large chamber tombs in the urban cemeteries of Portone, Badia, Ulimeto, Ripaie and Poggio alle Croci bear witness to the increase in the number of inhabitants and members of the different *gentes*. In the middle of the 4th cent. BC local craftsmen began to make red-figure pottery, a highly successful production that was to last for a century as is demonstrated by the numerous fine column kraters, or *kelebai*, that were exported to as far away as Latium, Umbria and the Po Valley. They were often intended right from the start

Left, two Volterran *kelebai* attributed to the Painter of the Pigmy, second half of the 4th cent. BC. Museo Archeologico, Colle di Val d'Elsa

Right, black-glaze krater, 4th-3rd cent. BC. Museo Etrusco Guarnacci, Volterra

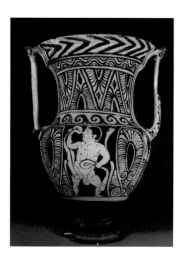

for use as cinerary urns. Even wider would be the diffusion, from the end of the century onward, of locally produced black-glaze ware: this type of pottery, developed in imitation of polished and burnished metal, was present on every Etruscan table for centuries, and was churned out by workshops organized along increasingly "industrial" lines, resulting in a marked decline in quality.

Equally important and familiar was the production of cinerary urns, which were made from limestone and tufa in the 4th and 3rd cent. BC. While the older types were chests with lids in the form of a pitched roof, reclining figures appeared on the lids as idealized representations of the deceased in the second half of the 4th century. Later the chests too would be ever more lavishly carved with

Top, casket urn,
4th cent. BC; above,
urn with reclining male
figure, 3rd cent. BC,
from the Volterran
region. Museo Etrusco
Guarnacci, Volterra

The Porta all'Arco,
3rd-2nd cent. BC

The Roman theater of Vallebuona, early 1st cent. AD

A section of mosaic from the baths near Vallebuona, 2nd-3rd cent. AD

scenes from mythology, or images of combat, travel or leave-taking, and some would be made of alabaster painted in a variety of colors, perhaps inspired by works of "major" sculpture from Rhodes or Pergamon. The oldest examples seem to indicate the presence of craftsmen from Southern Etruria, while in later periods there may have been an influx from Greece.

The economic development of the city prompted the construction of yet another circle of walls around the first half of the 3rd cent. BC. This enlargement of the urban area, bringing it to almost 120 hectares, resulted in the destruction of numerous buildings in what had previously been the suburbs as well as the older cemeteries, in a major work of demolition and reconstruction. Their place was taken by the houses of city dwellers, as well as by several areas that were left free as refuges where the inhabitants of the surrounding villages could gather with their livestock and chattels in times of conflict. Two gates were opened in this circle, Porta Diana and Porta all'Arco: the former originally had a wooden superstructure

set on top of two sturdy stone jambs and led from the city's main street to the routes for the valleys of the Elsa and Arno. The Porta all'Arco, located on the southern side, must once have had the same appearance but was subsequently (3rd-2nd cent. BC) modified to give it the form we see today. On the outside it has two pillars built out of squared blocks, topped by an arch with a span of over 4 m on which are set three human heads: now indecipherable, these may once have represented protective deities.

In the Hellenistic era the acropolis of Volterra was restructured, with the construction of two adjacent temples. All that remains of the older one to the north, dating from the 3rd cent. BC, is the base, but this is sufficient to make out its plan with a cell and *alae* preceded by two rows of four columns. The other place of worship, built in the 2nd cent. BC, was set on a tall podium with a flight of steps and had the appearance of a Greek temple, with a cell surrounded at the sides and rear by a colonnade. Parts of the decorative terracotta panels of both temples have been found inside the sacred precinct, or *temenos*. The area of the acropolis is now open to the public and can be reached from the fortress.

In 205 BC Volterra was one of the cities that supplied material for the fitting out of Scipio's fleet: its contribution of grain and timber bore witness to the fertility of the soil and abundance of the forests. Granted Roman citizenship in 90 BC, the Volterrans sided with Marius against Sulla, who besieged the city from 80 to 79 BC, resulting in capitulation, loss of citizenship and conversion of its territory into *ager publicus*. The grave crisis of the local aristocracy, some of whom had ties with the defeated faction, did not affect all the old Etruscan families: the Caecina (formerly Ceicna) retained a political and economic role, allowing them to finance the construction of the theater of Vallebuona (beginning of the 1st cent. AD), which entailed a modification of the urban structure of the surrounding district, and later on (2nd-3rd cent. AD) the city's baths.

The Late Settlements of the Territory

The Roman villa in the Archeological Park of San Vincenzino, near Cecina, is traditionally attributed to the Caecina as well. It is a building that came into existence (*c.* 30 BC) as a typical urban villa where oil was produced. The baths and summer *triclinium* were added later (2nd-3rd cent. AD). Evidence of life at the place, which remained inhabited up until the 5th cent. AD, is provided by the cemetery and small Antiquarium.

Various settlements in the coastal area date from the Hellenistic period, when Volterra was at its most prosperous, including those of Castiglioncello and Pian dei Lupi, which may have marked the northwest boundary of Volterran territory. The cemeteries of both have been found, and that of Castiglioncello comprised over three hundred tombs where the dead had often been buried, from the end of the 4th cent. BC onward, with goods characteristic of fighting men. It is likely, as a consequence, that the settlement was a military outpost of Pisa guarding the border with Volterra, as well as a secondary port used by ships sailing to Spain and Campania. The settlement reached the peak of its success in the 3rd and 2nd cent. BC, only to go into decline at the beginning of the 1st with changes in the road system and trade routes.

The oldest tombs of Pian dei Lupi, just north of Rosignano Marittimo where their contents are on display, date from the first half of the 3rd cent. BC. From these tombs come not only table pottery and precious objects in gold and silver, but also numerous weapons made of iron (spears, javelins, swords). These reflect a need for defense.

There is also evidence for the existence of many farming villages and fortified towns further inland. These settlements provided a constant source of commodities for Volterra, and at the same time an abiding market for its own handicrafts. Casole, in the upper valley of the Elsa, was an important settlement at the center of a series of minor sites, whose scattered tombs have been uncovered, along a route that linked them to the road leading from Monteriggioni to Volterra. Monteriggioni itself, with its extensive necropolis, bears witness to the vitality of these centers, occupied by wealthy aristocratic families like the Calisna Sepu, whose tomb was identified a century ago.

To the south of Volterra, at Sasso Pisano, an Etruscan complex of temples and baths has been excavated and can now be visited. Built in the 3rd cent. BC, it was restored after a landslide and then remained in use up until the 3rd cent. AD. The public importance of the place has suggested identification of the buildings with the Aquae Volaterranae marked on the *Peutinger Table*, a medieval copy of a map of the Roman empire.

The public complex of Torretta Vecchia near Collesalvetti can perhaps be identified with another site indicated on the *Peutinger Table*, the Mansio Turrita. It was continuously inhabited between the 1st cent. BC and the middle of the 6th cent. AD, with clearly recognizable remains of the Augustan era, including those of small heated baths. Abandoned in the middle of the 6th century, during the Gothic War, it can now be visited by prior arrangement. (M.M.)

Arms and the Army

In protohistoric times, when boundaries between communities were blurred and rights based on custom or force, the protection of groupings of human beings and their territory was one of the fundamental activities of collective life. In the communities of the early Iron Age, men qualified for the use of arms — by birth, age, physical strength and economic means — quickly became a special group, set apart by this activity for which they were required to acquire arms and sustenance during operations at their own expense. Entry into these armed bands was in all probability preceded by a process of initiation, of a religious and psychological character and possibly linked to hunting as well, that lasted for several years. So not all

Bronze bits from Accesa, second half of the 8th cent. BC. Museo Archeologico, Massa Marittima

Shield in bronze plate from the Petrina necropolis at Narce, first half of the 7th cent. BC. Museo Nazionale Etrusco di Villa Giulia, Rome

only risks but also palpable advantages, such as access to the politically active part of the community, the right to plunder and, very soon, a share in the appropriation of conquered land. As a consequence military activity always constituted an important recognition of social status among the Etruscans, inducing the classes that were excluded to demand, throughout the duration of their civilization, an extension of the right to take part in war.

In the Villanovan period the army was made up chiefly of young foot soldiers armed with short spears. The warriors used these weapons to strike the enemy with thrusts in the manner of a pike, or by throwing them from a very short distance. In the single combats into

which battles used to disintegrate after the first clash between ranks, the older fighters were given an advantage by their possession of short swords with triangular, ribbed blades. The wealthier would later (8th cent. BC) equip themselves with horses and chariots, from which they preferred to use the long sword with parallel edges called the "antennae" or "Tarquinia" type. The cavalry was undoubtedly the most effective strike force, capable of reversing the fortunes of any encounter and exercising control over areas at great distances. Consequently it enjoyed greater prestige and was the corps that gained the principal economic advantages from war.

To protect themselves warriors generally wore helmets made of leather and reinforced with metal studs, or completely covered with a layer of bronze and richly decorated in relief, as well as plumes or metal crests on top. As body armor they used corselets, again made of leather, with a metal

Italic sword with sheath from the necropolis of the Osteria at Vulci, 8th cent. BC. Museo Nazionale Etrusco di Villa Giulia, Rome

adult males attained the rank of warrior, and the process of training must have entailed further levels of distinction after the first rung, a hypothesis that is supported by the rarity of graves in which men were buried with swords rather than spears. From the archeological evidence, Latin literature and the *Iguvine Tables* (seven bronze tables found at Gubbio, describing the religious ceremonies of an Umbrian brotherhood), it appears that the military forces were divided into young men with or without spears, and mature men armed with swords or lacking them.

It is clear from the above that admission to the army was a mark of economic distinction, which brought not

Helmet with cheek guards from the necropolis of San Raffaele at Todi, first half of the 5th cent. BC. Museo Nazionale Etrusco di Villa Giulia, Rome

Villanovan crested helmet, first quarter of the 8th cent. BC. British Museum, London

plate at the center of the breast. Shields, like of those Homeric times and primitive peoples in general, were made of several layers of hide. Battles, where the elders led the young into combat, did not involve formations organized into orderly lines or complicated tactics: rather they were — if not straightforward ambushes — engagements with confused *mêlées* in which, after an exchange of javelins and hand-to-hand fighting, the winning side was able to pursue and slaughter the fleeing opponents,

invading and sacking their village. The strong influence exercised by the Orient on the art and material culture of Etruria from the second half of the 7th century onward extended to the organization of the army as well. In line with trends introduced from the Eastern Mediterranean increasing use was made of war chariots, ever more luxurious in appearance and faced with embossed sheets of bronze. In addition to transporting warriors, they proved an effective means of controlling outlying areas, and in any case were status symbols of great prestige. The ownership of horses had been a mark of socioeconomic distinction for some time, as these animals were not used in

farming. The Orientalizing period saw the importation of swift and nimble breeds that were particularly suited for use as cavalry mounts. Harnessed with finely decorated bits made of bronze, these horses were in some cases sacrificed on the death of their master, following him into the tomb in accordance with a custom that was also practiced on Cyprus.

The economic growth of the period also brought greater ostentation in the design of swords, made out of carburized iron (i.e. strengthened by the addition of carbon) and decorated with applications of gold, ivory and amber, and of shields, which became larger and were faced with sheets of

Detail of the Chigi Olpe from Veii representing two phalanxes of hoplites, second half of the 7th cent. BC. Museo Nazionale Etrusco di Villa Giulia, Rome

Warriors carrying a wounded companion, upper handle of a cist from Praeneste, early 4th cent. BC. Museo Nazionale Etrusco di Villa Giulia, Rome

bronze decorated in relief. Hellenic influence was also responsible for the adoption of the Corinthian helmet, which provided complete protection for the head with fixed coverings for the nose and cheeks. This was accompanied by the use of heavier armor and metal greaves for the legs. In addition, the contemporary organization of society into *gentes* formed the basis for a perfunctory ordering of the units and for their hierarchization, although the tactics adopted in battle remained simple and the size of armies fairly small, with considerable differences in the weaponry carried by their members, left to individual preference and funds.

A profound change took place over the course of the 6th century, when the social classes not permitted to bear

arms began to exert great pressure to be admitted to the ranks of the army and, accordingly, active political engagement in the community. In fact many people had grown sufficiently prosperous through farming or commerce for them to take on the obligations connected with military activity and at the same time aspire to play a role in government. A series of reforms – along the lines of the one launched in Rome by Servius Tullius – progressively introduced a division of the population into classes of wealth into the cities of Etruria. To some extent this opened up admission to the army to the lower strata of society, although the higher ranks were still recruited from the aristocracy. The consequent massive increase in the number of soldiers led to an

organization of the troops based on the Greek model of the phalanx of hoplites, i.e. rows of serried ranks in which each foot soldier – equipped with spear and shield identical to those of their comrades-in-arms – became a pawn in a complex strategy of battle drawn up by a sort of General Staff. Unlike in Greece, where the hoplites were armed in a standardized way, warriors in Etruria preserved a certain differentiation into corps, as can be seen for example from the five types of unit portrayed on the *situla* from the necropolis of the Certosa at Bologna. In general their equipment consisted of helmets with cheek guards, large round shields and long spears. Some warriors also carried a special single-edged sword with a curved blade, called a *machaira* and similar to the Greek *kopis*. Armor became more flexible and robust, thanks to the introduction of corselets made of plastered cloth and leather with fixed metal scales; in other cases, in imitation of the heroic nudity of the past, soldiers wore bronze cuirasses in two pieces that reproduced the anatomy of a powerful male torso. Thus the infantry took on the guise of a strictly regimented detachment, meeting the enemy attack in close ranks so that each warrior was able to use the large shield carried on his left arm partly to defend the man next to him. Among the later support units, it is worth mentioning the socially humble one of the slingsmen, who took part in operations from the margins of the battlefield. In fact they were equipped solely with slings made of cloth or leather and pieces of stone or metal for use as ammunition. The presence of these troops alongside the more or less heavily armored foot soldiers and the cavalry made the Etruscan armies complex and diversified forces with considerable fighting power, but they proved unable to stand up to the Roman legions. (M.M.)

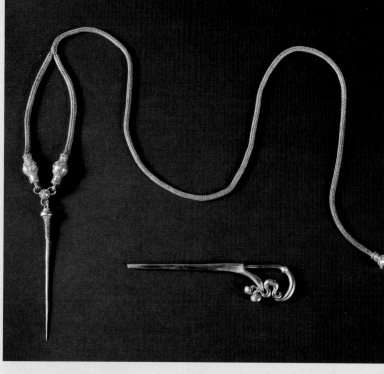

The Museo Etrusco "Guarnacci" in Volterra

One of the oldest public museums not just in Tuscany but in Europe, it is named after the abbé Mario Guarnacci, a priest and scholar who lived in Volterra in the middle of the 18th century (1701-85). The typical figure of a local man of learning, Guarnacci founded the museum in 1761, when his private collection had been considerably enlarged by the finds that he acquired from their chance discoverers or unearthed himself in the city.

Intended for public use by its proprietor, the museum immediately attracted the keen interest of scholars and has never ceased to be a point of reference for enthusiasts from all over the world. In fact it became, along with the city of Volterra, an obligatory stop on the Grand Tour.

Over the centuries the museum has been substantially enriched by groups of objects brought to light in new excavations, and as a result is today in a position to tell the whole story of Villanovan, Etruscan and Roman Volterra. Thus the stratification of the collections also reflects the cultural development of the history of archeology, with sections still in an antiquarian style and new areas that have a more modern focus on

Jewelry from Gesseri di Berignone near Volterra, 650-625 BC

Museum reconstruction of the Badia Tomb, second half of the 8th cent. BC

The *kyathos* of Monteriggioni with inscription, mid-7th cent. BC

education, where the objects are arranged in chronological succession. As a consequence a visit to the "Guarnacci" allows us to make a journey not just through the centuries, but also through the spirit that has determined the changing approach to research over time.

On the ground floor the opening section is devoted to the prehistoric and protohistoric periods (room I), with characteristic materials excavated in the Villanovan necropolises of the early Iron Age. These document the prosperity of the first Etruscan settlements and their distinctive production of pottery and metal ware. Of great evocative power, as well as scientific interest, is the chest tomb built out of stone slabs discovered in the necropolis of Badia and reconstructed in the museum along with its cinerary urn and grave goods, as is the "Q" Tomb with its terracotta jar. The material from the tomb of the Warrior at Poggio alle Croci, on display in the room on the right of the entrance, is also from the mature Villanovan period (mid-8th cent. BC). The grave contained a crested helmet and a metal flask formed from two pieces of bronze plate. The following room (II) houses materials of a later date, from the Orientalizing phase: outstanding among these are the pail or *kyathos* in *bucchero* from Monteriggioni, with a dedicatory inscription, and the jewelry from Gesseri di Berignone, unearthed in the 19th century. The stone stelae, on the other hand, date from the older phase of Etruscan Volterra: on that of the warrior Avile Tite the armed man is represented in a manner that was to inspire the sculpture produced at Fiesole. Another lofty example of archaic Volterran sculpture is the *Lorenzini Head* (room III), the oldest

religious statue in marble from Central Etruria. It probably depicts the god Apollo. A large number of chest-shaped cinerary urns from the Hellenistic period are also on display (rooms IV-IX), most of them carved from alabaster or tuff.

The whole of the second floor, as well as part of the ground floor, is devoted to the museum's original collection, completed around 1861 and systematically organized in 1877. In particular, rooms IV-XVIII house a large number of cinerary urns, around 600 in all, grouped by figurative themes. Even today they offer an unrivalled cross section of this class of products of the flourishing local handicrafts. The urns range from the simplest types, lacking figures and decorated with motifs in bas-relief, to more elaborate creations with the semi-recumbent figure of the

The stone stele of Avile Tite,
560 BC
A view of room VIII with
small figured cinerary urns

Small late Hellenistic urns
with the deceased husband
appearing to his wife,
and with Telephus in
the Greek camp

Small bronze called the
"Shadow of the Evening,"
3rd cent. BC

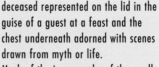

deceased represented on the lid in the
guise of a guest at a feast and the
chest underneath adorned with scenes
drawn from myth or life.

Much of the iconography of the smaller
urns reflects the popularity of Hellenic
myths, as well as Greek literature and
tragedy, while other figurations appear
to be related to local themes. In any
case, the scenes must have had an
allegorical and metaphorical
significance connected with the life of
the deceased.

Room XV catches our attention with the
Shadow of the Evening, as Gabriele
D'Annunzio dubbed the slender figure
of a youth: the name was later applied
to other votive bronzes of similar form.
According to one theory, its elongated
shape may be explained by the custom
of placing the statuettes in water and
the consequent need to compensate for
the optical effect of refraction, which
tends to make objects look squashed. It
is much more likely, however, that the
unusual dimensions of the ex-voto
stemmed from the client's desire to give
himself an impressive appearance: in

fact the figure is exactly two ancient
feet high and has the same weight as
ten one-as coins from the Etruscan mint
in Volterra.

Among the other celebrated pieces in
the museum is the lid of a terracotta
cinerary urn called the "Urn of the
Married Couple" (room XIX). It dates
from the beginning of the 1st cent. BC
but harks back in its modeling to older
sculptures; the vivid depiction of the
faces of the middle-aged husband and
wife has given rise to much debate over
the realism of the features reproduced.
Also on display on the second floor are
kraters, mirrors, votive bronze
offerings from Docciola (room XVII),
jewelry (room XVIII) and Roman
materials from the urban area and the
excavation of the theater at

Bronze coin with the inscription *Velathri* ("Volterra") and two-faced deities, 3rd cent. BC

Small late Hellenistic urn with Ulysses and the sirens

Armed and praying *kouroi*, late 7th cent. BC

Vallebuona, along with a rich collection of coins (room XXIII).

The third floor is occupied by a vast range of materials exemplifying the production of artistic handicrafts in the Hellenistic era. The current layout of the spaces places the emphasis on Etruscan burial complexes of recent acquisition, where the urn is shown in context with the other objects that accompanied it (rooms XXVII and XXVIII). The following rooms (XXXIII, XXXIV and XXVI) are dedicated to a selection of bronzes, while room XXXV

houses the famous statue of a woman with a newborn child known as the "Maffei *kourotrophos.*" Dating from the 3rd cent. BC, it may have come from a place of worship at Vallebuona. The last rooms contain red-figure vases (including the kraters, or *kelebai,* used as cinerary urns in the Hellenistic period), black-glaze pottery and a life-size reconstruction of the tomb of the Doorway (late 3rd – mid-2nd cent. BC). (M.M.)

On the left, column krater attributed to the Painter of Hesione, 330-310 BC; right, kalyx krater attributed to the Master of Montebradoni, last decades of the 4th cent. BC

pp. 188-9: detail of the lid of a cinerary urn called the "Urn of the Married Couple," early 1st cent. BC

BETWEEN THE ARNO AND THE APENNINES

The vast expanse of the middle valley of the Arno, flanked by the chain of the Apennines, was long thought to have been thinly populated in pre-Roman times, largely because of the presumed frequency of flooding along the course of the Arno and the extensive areas of marshland that would have made much of the plain unsuitable for permanent occupation.

In reality, the results of the archeological excavations carried out in the historic center of Florence in the 1980s (principally under Piazza della Signoria) have provided evidence for a very early frequentation of the site, which played a crucial part in the system of communications owing to the ease with which the Arno River could be forded at this point.

Excavations in the area of Sesto Fiorentino have also shown that the broad plain to the west of Florence has been permanently inhabited since the Neolithic, and that numerous villages existed during the Copper and Bronze Age too. Far from representing an obstacle to settlement, the abundance of water that characterized the environment favored agricultural activities, as well as stock raising and fishing, which was practiced in the huge lakes fed by the rivers.

Prehistory at Sesto Fiorentino and in the Mugello

To understand the human occupation of this area we need to see the presence of settlements on high ground in relation to those in the valleys. In fact humankind first appeared in the region around Scandicci (Monte Lepri, Bricoli) over 100 000 years ago, and numerous finds in the Mugello, some of them along the course of the Sieve, also date from the Paleolithic. Various phases of the Neolithic are documented at several sites on the Sesto plain, but their number increased further in the Copper Age, both in its earliest phases and in that of what is known as the "Bell-Beaker Culture," which spread throughout Europe in the second half of the 3rd millennium BC. Moreover, the growth of population in the settlements of the Sesto region (there were around fifteen of them on the shores of the large lake) is matched by the frequency of finds in other parts of the territory, such as Fiesole and the Mugello. Analysis of the location of the Chalcolithic finds allows us to identify the routes across the Apennines: through the valley of the Marina and the pass of Vetta

alle Croci di Calenzano, people from the Sesto area were able to enter into contact with Emilia, and by following the course of the Arno and ascending the Sieve, they could cross the Muraglione Pass and reach the valley of the Montone in Romagna. From Borgo San Lorenzo, again following the Sieve, a route passing through Ronta led to Marradi and then over the Apennines through the valley of the Lamone; ascending the Stura from Barberino, traders could use the Raticosa Pass. Among other things, these contacts by land, some of them over long distances, provides an explanation for the shapes and distinctive geometric decoration of Chalcolithic pottery, just as the utilization of the course of the Arno for communications explains affinities with the lower Valdarno and Versilia, as well as with the upper Valdarno.

During the Bronze Age, and especially its middle phase, there was a profound change in the nature of handicrafts and the economy, and even in the location of settlements. More and more objects were made out of metal instead of stone, people chose to raise goats and sheep rather than cattle and various villages began to appear on the reliefs and their lower slopes, as happened in the Prato region, for reasons that can perhaps be ascribed to environmental factors, although conflict with other human groups may have played a part.

This was also the moment when the settlement located at Fiesole developed and became permanent. Traces of it have been found on the elevation of San Francesco and on its eastern slopes, in the area of the Etruscan temple.

Through the settlements that attest to the most recent and final phase of the Bronze Age, we come to the Iron Age, with the oldest Etrus-

can stages of Villanovan culture. These are documented in various localities, although they seem to reflect a peopling of the area that was widespread but not substantial: on top of the finds at Neto di Dogaia on the Sesto plain come those of Santa Lucia, Val di Rose and Madonna del Piano, with groups of graves that are mostly of the "well" type, containing cremated bodies. Other traces have been found at nearby Castellina in Quinto Fiorentino. At the locality of Palastreto, on the lower slopes of Monte Morello, about twenty well tombs have been brought to light: partly excavated out of the rock, they held materials from the late Villanovan period and the subsequent Orientalizing phase.

The Origins of Florence

All these small groups of tombs undoubtedly belonged to scattered settlements of a family character, perhaps "federated" in some way. A similar situation has been identified in the center of Florence, where six well tombs with biconical jars and vases from the 8th cent. BC were discovered in the 19th century, and where more recently other finds from destroyed graves have been made, alongside

fragments of pottery with geometric decoration imported from Greece or Southern Italy. The provenance of these last finds is a clear indication of the role of commercial junction that the Florentine settlement represented at its origins, as a useful crossroads on the routes between Northern Etruria and the Apennine passes. Confirmation of this is provided by the presence in Florence and Volterra of *fibulae*

Jar with cinerary urn from tomb 6 of the Gambrinus Necropolis at Florence, mid-8th cent. BC. Museo di Firenze com'era, Florence

Cinerary urn with bowl-lid from the tomb 4 of the Gambrinus Necropolis at Florence, mid-8th cent. BC. Museo di Firenze com'era, Florence

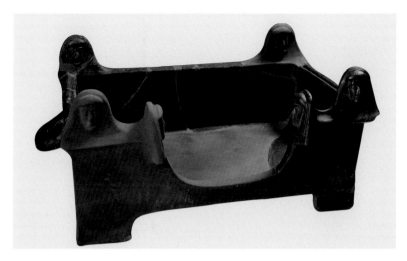

Bucchero *foculus* made at
Chiusi, from Via Strozzi
in Florence, second half
of the 6th cent. BC.
Museo di Firenze com'era,
Florence

Small bronze of a warrior
from the center
of Florence, second half
of the 6th cent. BC.
Museo di Firenze com'era,
Florence

Cippus from Via dei Bruni
in Florence, mid-6th cent.
BC. Museo di Firenze
com'era, Florence

decorated with pieces of amber that must have
arrived from Central Europe through the
Mugello and the valley of the Reno, and by the
characteristics of the finds made in the Florentine territory, plainly influenced by those of
the Bolognese and Volterran regions. With
these areas, in addition, it shares the persistence of aspects of Villanovan culture up until
the third quarter of the 7th cent. BC; typical
examples are the crude *impasto* jars decorated
with applied cords, which in the territory of
Volterra and the region around Florence were
used both for household purposes and to hold
the ashes from cremations.

Some remains found sporadically in excavations, or reused in constructions, date from
more recent times (6th cent. BC); these are materials relating to burials that indicate an Etruscan presence in the Archaic era. They include
a fragment of *bucchero* ware with the earliest
Etruscan inscription from the Florentine area,
brought to light not long ago. For more unequivocal documentation of the past of Florence, however, it is necessary to wait for the birth of the
Roman colony of Florentia, founded in 59 BC
according to the Latin sources. Yet archeological
excavations in the city have shown clearly that,
while the *Lex* determining the creation of the
city was approved on that date, the actual foundation did not take place before 30-15 BC, and
thus during the reign of Octavian Augustus. The
forum was located on the site of what is now Piazza della Repubblica, baths and laundries occupied Piazza Signoria, while the remains of the
theater are located under Palazzo Vecchio; the
city walls passed immediately behind. There is
an accurate reconstruction of the topography
of Roman Florence in the Museo di Firenze
com'era, together with a selection of the materials uncovered.

Quinto Fiorentino

The entrance *dromos* and pillar of the central chamber of the Montagnola Tomb at Quinto Fiorentino, late 7th cent. BC

While the residential area of the Early Iron Age and Orientalizing phase at Quinto Fiorentino has been identified only hypothetically, two monumental chamber tombs constructed out of blocks of stone and surmounted by an enormous mound of earth have survived. The more intact of the two, the Montagnola Tomb, has a diameter of about 60 m, and is ringed by a drum of stone slabs with a circumference of 125 m. A long open passageway – or *dromos* – leads to the inner vestibule through a portal formed of two monoliths acting as jambs and one as a lintel. The walls of the rectangular vestibule, originally plastered and painted brown, blue and red, still have graffiti with stars, animals, plants and letters; here, at the sides, were set the doors of two small cells. The roof of the vestibule was built using the technique of corbelling, which preceded the introduction of the arched vault. This entailed laying rows of stones that projected further and further out from the side walls until they touched in the middle, resulting in a solid roof with two pitches. A pointed doorway at the back of the vestibule leads to the circular cell, also roofed with a corbel vault; the sturdy central pillar still bears inscriptions and nails from which some elements of the grave goods were hung. Looted in antiq-

uity, the Tomb of the Montagnola has unfortunately only yielded a few fragmentary remains of its original contents. However, these are sufficient to demonstrate that they were extremely rich, and must have included an iron bed, spits, knives, and dining implements. There were also many exotic objects made of ivory and bone, alabaster *unguentaria* along with a glass *aryballos* from Egypt, decorated ostrich eggs from the East and pieces of amber from Central Europe. On top of all this there were bronze, silver and gold ware of Etruscan production, as well as *bucchero* vessels and Etruscan-Corinthian pottery, offering a chronological horizon spanning the end of the 7th and the beginning of the 6th cent. BC.

A short distance away stands the tomb of the Mula, now underneath the villa of the same name, of which it forms the cellar. Discovered a very long time ago, its contents have unfortunately vanished, but the innermost part of the original vestibule (now connected to a modern staircase) has been preserved, along with a majestic portal that leads into the round cell with a diameter of 9 m, lacking a central pillar perhaps since ancient times.

While no more than a few stones remain of other, similar tombs in Quinto, contemporary tombs have been found at the nearby locality of Palastreto. These are still of the "well" type, with ribbed vases containing the grave goods, some of considerable value. The survival of this type of container in the funerary ritual is of great significance, for it shows that, notwithstanding the diffusion of chamber tombs used for the multiple burials of members of rich clans uniting more than one family, the practice of individual burial was maintained by people less influenced by the organization of society into *gentes*, but faithful to the cultural tradition of protohistoric origin.

There was a very similar situation in the Mugello, where archeological research has been resumed in recent years with considerable success, as the exhibitions staged at the museums of Bruscoli, Palazzuolo sul Senio and Sant'Agata demonstrate. Without listing

The interior of the tomb of the Mula at Quinto Fiorentino, late 7th cent. BC

the many sporadic finds, it will suffice to mention those of the settlement at Poggio di Colla near Vicchio and San Piero a Sieve. A settlement existed at the first locality as early as the 7th cent. BC and, with the addition of a temple and sacred area (6th cent. BC) as well as a cemetery with burial mounds, lasted right up to the Hellenistic period. At the second, besides the remains of a chamber tomb from the first half of the 6th cent. BC, a necropolis from an earlier period has been identified, adjoining an area used for the production of pottery and the working of metal, from which it is separated by a wall embellished with antefixes and painted tiles. The type of burial practiced in the 7th century, in well tombs, indicates a clear survival of protohistoric cultural patterns, but the number of graves and the size of the adjacent pottery suggest a populous and well-organized community.

Artimino and Comeana

More discoveries of great importance have been made at Artimino, where an elevation with three small but distinct summits was the site of a settlement as far back as the 7th cent. BC. In addition to finds from the inhabited area, located during the Orientalizing period in the area of the *Paggeria* or Servants' Quarters of the Medici villa, there are the remains of tombs from the cemeteries at Prato di Rosello and Comeana. Various tombs from the most recent Orientalizing phase, spanning the 7th and 6th cent. BC, have been identified in the former. They include Tumulus C, with a diameter of 30 m, which has a passageway and internal cell looted in antiquity, as well as a paved altar-terrace for exposition of the deceased and the grave goods. It was probably created at the same time as the first version of the mound, which later collapsed and was reconstructed. From this tomb comes a splendid *bucchero* incense burner on a tall foot, fitted with two movable arms supporting containers in the form of a truncated cone, with a boat-

Sword with sheath and head of large spear; bronze cinerary urn from the tomb of the Warrior at Prato di Rosello, Artimino, 8th-7th cent. BC. Museo Archeologico, Artimino

Reconstruction of the tomb of the Warrior at Prato di Rosello, Artimino, 8th-7th cent. BC. Museo Archeologico, Artimino

Bucchero censer from Tumulus C of the necropolis of Prato di Rosello, last two decades of the 7th-early 6th cent. BC. Museo Archeologico, Artimino

shaped receptacle at the center; the inscription engraved on the foot tells us that the object belonged to Larthuza Kuleniie.

The characteristics and state of preservation of this tomb mean that it cannot be visited, unlike the nearby Tumulus A, where a cremation burial from the end of the 6th cent. BC was discovered. In the vicinity stands Tumulus B from the middle of the 7th cent. BC, whose drum was protected by stones and a sort of "eave" made of slabs; a passageway that was probably uncovered led in the past to a rectangular space divided by a pillar, used to support the horizontal slabs that formed the ceiling. The remains of an older grave (8th-7th cent. BC) of the well type have also been found

Amphora with lid
from the Boschetti Tomb,
670-650 BC. Museo
Archeologico, Artimino

The two chambers
of the Boschetti Tomb at
Comeana, 670-650 BC

The entrance of the most
recent tomb of the
Montefortini Tumulus,
last quarter of the
7th cent. BC

in this tomb. The intact grave goods are those of a warrior of the dominant class, and include a large spear, a short sword, a bronze breastplate and vessels made of bronze plate and fired clay.

Along an ancient road on the plain beneath is set the necropolis of Comeana, housing the tombs of wealthy landowners, in an area of thriving agricultural settlements. The Boschetti Tomb, now open to the public, consisted of a short passageway that led to a vestibule and an almost cubic space of 2 m on a side. Similar to the tombs at Prato Rosello, it has yielded the scanty remains of at least two burials, including that of a rich warrior who lived around 670-650 BC.

The Montefortini Tumulus, on the other hand, has the proportions of an artificial hill. Over 60 m in diameter and about 15 high, it is supported by a drum of stones that is only partially visible, from which an altar-terrace projected for the exposition of the dead and their grave goods. The mound contains two tombs from different times, one of them open to the public. The oldest, dating from the mid-7th century, is located at the center of the mound and, like the Montagnola Tomb at Quinto, has a circular cell with a corbelled vault. It has a diameter of over 7 m and a central pillar. At the time of its discovery the vestibule was still closed by the original slab of stone, while the access corridor had been destroyed by the construction of the second tomb: it appears in fact, from the signs left by the collapse of the vaults of the older tomb, that the monument had been irreparably damaged in an earthquake. So the new tomb, now accessible, was created in the place of the corridor, preceded by a 13-m-long open passageway and a vestibule covered with projecting stones. These lead, through a movable door that has now vanished, to a rectangular cell over 4 m long, also covered with a corbeled vault and fitted with the same stone "shelf" running around the walls as is the older, circular *tholos*.

Despite being plundered in antiquity, this tomb, like the inner one, has yielded precious fragments of ivories, gold work and local and foreign (including Egyptian) pottery that allow us to date it to the last quarter of the 7th century.

All in all, therefore, it is clear that this intensively farmed area was at the hub of growing commercial and cultural exchanges, whose effects on protohistoric traditions led to the belated (and initially not accepted by all) introduction of models of princely life of Oriental origin, along with the organization of the population into *gentes*, i.e. groups of families descended from a single common ancestor. The *gens* constituted the basis of the inheritance of land and wealth, and the large monumental tombs that each *gens* erected for itself were an unambiguous mark of prosperity and dominion of the territory. The increase in the number of settlements and their aggregation from the end of the 7th century onward was a prelude in some places, such as Fiesole and Artimino, to the formation of urban structures, as the emergence of types of handicraft aimed at extensive markets also seems to indicate. Thus the northern inland region of Etruria exhibits in this phase a blend of tradition and innovation that constitutes the distinctive feature of a fairly large and culturally homogeneous area.

The Formation of the First Urban Center at Fiesole

The stele of Larth Ninie from the environs of Fiesole, last decades of the 6th cent. BC. Casa Buonarroti, Florence

Sandstone stele from Travignoli near Fiesole, early 5th cent. BC. Museo Archeologico, Fiesole

In the Early Iron Age Fiesole appears to have still been occupied by small villages, probably located on the two summits of the hill and on the level ground in the middle. Several holes in the rock and a rectangular hollow have been identified in the strata under the Etruscan temple, perhaps connected with huts of the Villanovan period rather than burials. From the same area, although lacking their original context, come numerous remains of both Villanovan and Orientalizing pots, including distinctive two-horned handles with hollow appendages, common in inland Etruria and Emilia, as well as fragments of ribbed vases of the type already referred to, found in many areas of inland Etruria. These finds are displayed in the local Museo Civico Archeologico, located in the area of the excavations, where it is also possible to visit the remains of the Etruscan temple of the Hellenistic era, the baths, the theater and the temple of the Roman era.

The pottery of the Orientalizing period unearthed at Fiesole should be seen in relation to the remains of buildings that were destroyed by the subsequent creation of a sacred area but which are recognizable as dwellings. They may have been used in the final part of the 7th century, i.e. the period in which the entire Florentine region seems to have gone through a phase of demographic and economic growth closely linked with the increase in trade on the various lines of communication.

Fiesole can be seen as a paradigmatic example of the process of formation of the pre-urban centers of North Etruria, destined to thrive with the passing of the centuries. Here, with the beginning of the 6th cent. BC, we see an exponential increase in the quantity of finds, as well as a radical change in their typology. But it is the level of finishing and the uniformity of these pots, made on the wheel from clay of high quality, that clearly show them to be the products of true workshops of craftsmen, whose existence presupposes the presence of a large number of people, i.e. a substantial and enduring demand. The occupation of the whole area of the modern town is

confirmed by the diffuse presence of pottery from the period, and by the identification of the remains of several buildings under the temple laid out in parallel and orthogonal lines, which suggests some sort of embryonic planning. In any case Fiesole was, in the early 6th cent. BC, a social structure made up of a large number of individuals occupying a very large area, and living in houses on a quadrangular plan.

The population produced specialized goods (such as stelae, sculptures and *bucchero* ware) which were marketed in surrounding communities as well, through the use of means of

communication whose importance was to grow in the middle of the 6th century, in concomitance with the colonization of the Po Valley.

It was in the middle of that century that the part of Fiesole on the northeast slopes of the main hill underwent a profound restructuring, perhaps following a fire whose origin cannot be determined. After that event a sacred area was created with a small, almost square place of worship at its center. About 5 m on a side, it had walls of unbaked bricks set on stone podia. It had a simple earthen floor but the roof was tiled and had painted antefixes and *acroteria* at the ends of the crossbeam, decorated with a carved seahorse. A drain, a few terraces and areas of paving completed the area; also linked with it were a sculpture of a crouching lion in *pietra serena* (perhaps part of an altar or an architectural element) and a stone plinth, as well as miniature pots made of black and gray *bucchero*, Attic vases and small votive bronzes.

Another small building of sacred use erected in the 5th century and renovated during the Hellenistic era was present on the southern side of Fiesole, near Villa Marchi. Over forty votive bronzes were found in its area, along with pottery and fragments of *aes rude* (lumps of bronze used as currency before the introduction of coins). The presence of a stone sculpture of a lion, Archaic and miniature pottery and a helmet with a carinate cap on the hill of San Francesco suggests that there was a place of worship with votive deposits here too, as well as on the eastern elevation (Sant'Apollinare) from where come a refined bronze rep-

Stone lion's head from the acropolis of Fiesole, 6th-5th cent. BC. Museo Etnografico Missionario, Fiesole

Small votive bronze from the deposit at Villa Marchi, first half of the 5th cent. BC. Museo Archeologico, Fiesole

Structures of the Etruscan acropolis in the Museo Etnografico Missionario at Fiesole, 5th-4th cent. BC

Bronze helmet from the acropolis of Fiesole, first half of the 5th cent. BC. Museo Etnografico Missionario, Fiesole

resenting Heracles dressed in the skin of the Nemean lion. This set of roughly contemporary *sacella* seems to be related to the definition of the urban area, as the sacred areas that have been identified with precision are adjacent to the route later followed by the city walls, built for reasons of security perhaps from the 5th century onward.

The walls form an impressive line of defense running for 2.5 km, still visible despite their demolition by the Florentines in 1125. The longest surviving parts are on the northern and eastern sides, but shorter stretches are also present to the south and on the citadel.

The city's craft workshops were in all likelihood responsible for a type of figured stele carved from *pietra serena*. Known as *pietre fiesolane*, they are present throughout the territory stretching from the Mugello to the valleys of the Sieve, Arno and Greve, and as far as Prato and Pistoia. It is these stele that best document the development of Etruscan settlements in the area of Florence, Prato and Pistoia from the years at the turn of the 6th and 5th century onward. While the sculptures found at Fiesole indicate the city's central role in the production of these works, certain iconographic features that can be discerned in them reflect the cultural influences of the time, coming from Volterra and Chiusi.

Gonfienti

The city that has only recently been identified on the Prato plain, at Gonfienti, should perhaps be seen in connection with the expansion of the Etruscan center of Clusium (Chiusi) into the Po Valley. The settlement, which is still being studied, was brought to light by chance during the construction of the freight exchange facility for Central Tuscany at the confluence of the Marina and Bisenzio. Covering at least 9 hectares, it was made up of large houses arranged in a grid of blocks, and without question laid out according to a systematic plan. Its chronology, centering on the 5th cent. BC, corresponds substantially with that of Marzabotto, a perhaps almost "mirror" city on the banks of the Reno on the other side of the Apennines, which was also founded during the historical period of Etruscan expansion to the north.

The Pressure of the Celts and Romanization

The altar and, below, the remains of the Etruscan temple, 4th-3rd cent. BC

At the end of the 6th cent. BC, while the influence of the Celts was growing in Central Europe, the Etruscans found it increasingly difficult to maintain their control of the Central Mediterranean. It was not long before Syracuse got the better of the Tyrrhenian navy, inflicting a crushing defeat on it at the battle of Cumae in 474 BC. As a consequence the cities of inland Etruria began to look for alternative routes of expansion across the Apennines, coming into contact with the coastal centers of the Northern Adriatic, where merchants from Attica had established a presence. This resulted in a rapid transformation of the areas of the Po Valley colonized by the Etruscans, which experienced a cultural as well as demographic spurt of growth that is reflected in the creation of cities like Marzabotto, systematically laid out in a grid in the manner typical of a colony. Gonfienti, for its part, must have been another product of this movement of expansion, so an investigation of its decline may help to clarify the picture of the regression of the whole of Northern Etruria under the impact of Celtic pressure from the north.

In fact the context of the region of Florence and the Mugello in this period is a fairly organic one. Whereas the majority of sites had not previously had significant defensive structures, at the settlements of Poggio di Colla and Frascole in the Mugello, dating from this period, sturdy stone walls were erected even around small villages or simple strongholds built on elevations as lookout posts.

The ring of walls around Artimino also seems to date from this time, preceding the Etruscan loss of control over the road that passed through this area from Pisa to Spina, i.e. linking the ports of the Tyrrhenian and the Adriatic. A 300-m stretch of this road has recently been uncovered at Casa del Lupo near Capannori. As has already been suggested, the construction of Fiesole's walls must have been a response to an urgent need for defense, even though the concentration of the population at this protected site had resulted in a growth of the city's economy, with local manufacturing activities taking the place of trade with the outside world.

The destruction of the northern *sacellum* of Fiesole by a fire, around the middle of the 5th

The steps of the Roman temple, third quarter of the 1st cent. BC

cent. BC, may have been followed shortly afterward by the construction of the large Etruscan temple, which can now be visited in the archeological area. The chronology of this building, traditionally dated to the end of the 4th century, is now undergoing revision. During its erection efforts were made not to desecrate the remains of the small shrine, over which the innermost cell of the new temple was situated. It had a larger cell at the center and two narrower rooms at the sides, the *alae*, while the walls extended as far as the building's façade. Thus its pronaos was closed at the sides, with only two columns of large size on the front. The complex was set on a tall podium, from which a flight of steps led down to the altar in front. Unlike the majority of Etruscan temples, the one in Fiesole had walls built of stone instead of unfired brick, which has allowed more of it to survive. Protected from the infiltration of water by a complicated system of drains that discharged outside the city, the temple was embellished in successive phases by a pediment with scenes of combat and lateral antefixes with small applied heads (3rd-2nd cent. BC), as well as two rooms located symmetrically at the sides. These were used to receive worshipers, who left small bronzes and pottery as votive offerings. The six Etruscan tombs in the only cemetery to have been identified in the city, on Via del Bargellino, also belong to this historical phase: dating from the end of the 4th century and reutilized up until the period of Romanization, only four of them are still visible.

Once again it was a great fire that brought this temple to the end of its existence, perhaps during the destruction of the city in 90 BC, which was followed in 80 by the founding of a Roman colony on the site by Sulla's veterans. The area of the Etruscan temple was buried under several meters of earth, and a new but larger building created on a similar plan to the previous one, endowed with a grand flight of steps and a colonnaded portico. Slightly more recent are the nearby theater, the baths and the structures brought to light between Via Pascoli and the seat of the Collezione Archeologica Costantini, apparently those of a public building.

The massive expropriations of land at the expense of the Etruscans and the concentration of activities in the new Romanized cities (such as Florentia in the plain beneath) resulted in the decline of many of the preexisting minor centers, along with a transformation of the roles played by several important Etruscan *gentes*. (M.M.)

The complex of the Roman baths, last quarter of the 1st cent. BC

Textiles and Clothing

Although the Etruscan woman played an important role in society and enjoyed considerable privileges in the classical era in comparison to what was permitted by the Greek or Latin tradition, she was always bound to the domestic sphere. In particular, it was customary for the true matron to spend her time spinning or weaving. This is confirmed by the contents of women's graves, which include simple tools used for spinning.

Just as was still the practice in the countryside up until the middle of the last century, the wool, wound round a distaff, was turned into yarn by twisting it with the aid of a wooden stick made to turn on its axis by a spherical counterweight made of fired clay, called a whorl. The loom, usually portable and fairly narrow although some very large ones also existed, was made of wood, which explains the absence of complete examples. What have survived, however, are the terracotta weights in the shape of a truncated pyramid, used to keep the warp taught, and a number of images, such as the one on a famous bronze pendant from Bologna or the one carved on the back of the wooden

throne from Tomb Lippi 89 at Verucchio. Recent studies have identified different levels of social status, and thus of skill, between the women buried with implements used for spinning rather than weaving. It can be inferred that the simpler activity of spinning was carried out by a very large number of women while the greater complexity

Buckle of man's belt from the western necropolis of Accesa Lake, last decades of the 7th cent. BC. Museo Archeologico, Massa Marittima

Sandals with wooden soles from the necropolis of the Olmo Bello at Bisenzio, late 6th cent. BC. Museo Nazionale Etrusco di Villa Giulia, Rome

Detail of women's footwear from the "Sarcophagus of the Married Couple" from Caere, second half of the 6th cent. BC. Museo Nazionale Etrusco di Villa Giulia, Rome

inherent in the transformation of yarn into cloth demanded more specific and developed capacities. A similar organization of labor survived for millennia in the Tuscan countryside, where until the 20th century only one of the old women in a small farming community was entrusted with the responsibility for commencing the warping of a piece of cloth on the loom.

Traditionally the garments formed out of simple drapes (tunic, or chiton, and

Pin with chain, second half of the 7th cent. BC. Museo Civico Archeologico delle Acque, Chianciano Terme

Bronze woman's belt from Tomb 543 of the Benacci burial ground in Bologna, 8th cent. BC. Museo Civico, Bologna

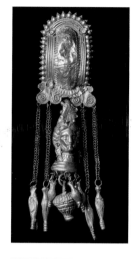

mantle) were fastened with metal *fibulae*, sometimes made of gold or silver, similar in shape to today's safety pins. The arch of the brooch took a variety of ornamental forms, often derived from the protohistoric tradition. In common use, at different times and places, were *fibulae* with simple (i.e. semicircular) arches or arches shaped like a violin bow (i.e. straight) or leech (bulging in the middle), with disk-shaped catch plates (i.e. with a metal disk holding the pin) and with inserts of precious materials, such as amber. Wealthier Etruscan women also wore gold jewelry – adorning their necks, ears and clothing – made by extremely sophisticated techniques that have already been discussed. Earrings in particular, from the Orientalizing period onward, displayed a great variety of form and ornamentation, from the simplest rings worn through the lobe to earrings with pendants, rosettes, and "cages." Following Greek fashions, the 4th century saw a diffusion of "cluster" earrings, earrings made of curved tubes terminating in the head of an animal and earrings with pendants of precious stones.

Men too wore tunics and cloaks, although from the 7th cent. BC onward the younger ones adopted very brief and close-fitting shorts. Also known are blouses resembling T-shirts, worn as the sole garment while working. Cloaks were fastened on the right shoulder – during the 7th and 6th centuries – by clasps, generally made of precious metal, with ornamental patterns on the visible part or decorated with figures in relief.

As far as footwear is concerned, boots of soft leather tied with laces and with a tongue covering the front of the shin were particularly popular among men over the course of the 6th and 5th centuries. Called *calcei repandi* and sought-after outside Etruria as well for their comfort and the elegant colors in which they were decorated, they ended in a characteristic raised tip like the shoes still worn on the southern and eastern shores of the Mediterranean. Less elegant – although the majority of the population often went barefoot – were the clogs with wooden soles and leather uppers or laces, the ancestors of various types of footwear in use in the countryside of Central Italy up until the 20th century. In some cases, as a number of finds has demonstrated, the rigidity of the wooden sole was reduced by inserting a metal hinge between the front and back parts, allowing the shoe to bend with the foot.

Among the accessories of symbolic value, the *lituus* had a special role in the religious and political sphere. This was a staff whose upper part was

Gold hair clip in the form of a comb from Praeneste, first half of the 7th cent. BC. Museo Nazionale Etrusco di Villa Giulia, Rome

curved like a crosier, carried by priests and, at times, other people of high rank. A symbol of authority, it was also the instrument used by the augur to subdivide the heavenly vault into sectors prior to the ceremonial reading of auspices, in line with the ritual laid down by tradition and in the scriptures. The ceremonial dress of the augur was completed by a conical hat and a short mantle fastened with a *fibula*, evidently based on an archaizing style. (M.M.)

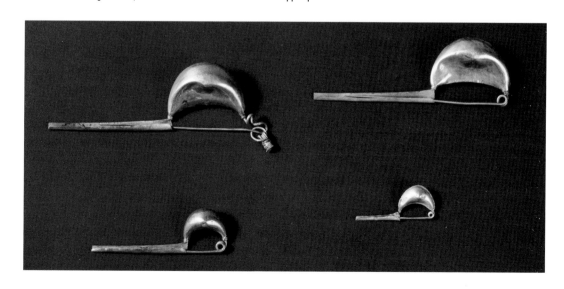

It was the first national archeological museum to be set up after the unification of Italy, in 1870; ten years after its creation it was moved to its current location, the 17th-century Palazzo della Crocetta, not far from Brunelleschi's celebrated Ospedale degli Innocenti.

Formed from the collections amassed by the Medici and the grand dukes, which included large Etruscan and Roman bronzes and gemstones, the Florentine museum has been used to conserve materials found all over the territory of Tuscany ever since it opened. However, there has not always been enough space to put them all on display. It also houses a prestigious Egyptian collection that is second in Italy only to the one in Turin. Created from an existing group of works assembled under Medici rule, it was significantly enriched by Grand Duke Leopold II of Lorraine, who went so far as to finance a scientific expedition to Egypt (1828-29).

On the ground floor, where temporary exhibitions are also staged, and outside the rooms that once housed the topographic section, there is an interesting garden laid out in a typically antiquarian style. Underneath the numerous varieties of tree and flowers with which it is planted, in fact, lie genuine Etruscan tombs – such as the one in an Oriental style from Casale Marittimo, dismantled and then reconstructed here – as well as reproductions of graves like the Inghirami Tomb in Volterra. Other features include the tomb of the Little Devil and the front of a small temple, inspired by the shrine of Ponte Rotto near Vulci, as well as smaller tombs

and numerous sculptures.

The second story of the building now houses both the Egyptian Museum, with new rooms in which the works have been arranged chronologically and, as far as possible, topographically, and the section of Etruscan and Roman sculpture in stone and bronze. The corridor linking the building with the right-hand aisle of the church of the Santissima Annunziata displays a collection of glyptics, with cameos from the Roman and Renaissance periods. This corridor ends in a fascinating raised alcove from which Cosimo II's sister Maria Maddalena de' Medici, "ill-formed of limb," could attend religious services held in the Florentine basilica without being seen.

The Etruscan collection commences in room XIV, the so-called Gallery of Bronzes; outstanding among these, in addition to numerous votive statuettes, are the large bronzes brought to light in the 16th century, formerly the pride of the Medicean collection. The first of them is the *Chimera* from Arezzo dating

from the 4th cent. BC. Discovered in 1553, its serpent's tail is the fruit of a restoration traditionally attributed to Benvenuto Cellini, although without any hard evidence. The large sculpture must once have been part of a group, of which the part made up of the winged horse ridden by Bellerophon has been lost, while the inscription on the monster's right paw tells us that the work was a votive offering to Jupiter-Tinia.

A short distance away stands the statue of an orator known as the *Arringatore* from Sanguineto sul Trasimeno, brought to Tuscany in an adventurous fashion following its discovery in 1566. Cast between 100 and 80 BC, in an already

The *Chimera of Arezzo*, 4th cent. BC

Opposite, detail of the *Minerva of Arezzo*, Roman copy of Praxiteles's original

On the left, small bronze representing Heracles from Poggio Castiglione near Massa Marittima, *circa* 300 BC; right, small bronze representing Laran, 475-450 BC

Statue of an orator called the *Arringatore* from Sanguineto sul Trasimeno, 100-80 BC

highly Romanized period, it bears an inscription in Etruscan on the lower edge of the tunic with the name of the person represented, Aule Meteli, and a dedication to a deity. The last of these masterpieces of Etruscan bronze sculpture is the *Minerva*, found near the church of San Lorenzo at Arezzo in 1541; completed with parts in plaster after its discovery and given a new right arm in bronze in the 18th century, it has recently undergone major restoration, like the rest of the sculptures in the room.

The following room (XV) houses other artifacts made of bronze, including oil lamps, weights, ornamental elements, a container-measure with a capacity of one *modius*, weapons of offense and

defense from various periods and Etruscan mirrors decorated with figures on the back. On the same story there are rooms displaying Etruscan stone sculptures, with small chest-shaped cinerary urns, sarcophagi (including that of the "Obese Etruscan"), cinerary statues and the pediment of a rock tomb from Norchia. Outstanding among these exhibits is the celebrated "Sarcophagus of the Amazons" from Tarquinia, recently subjected to careful restoration: carved by a Hellenic sculptor, probably around 375 BC, it was imported into Etruria and used to house the mortal remains of the noblewoman Ramtha Huzcnai. The

Detail of the "Sarcophagus of the Obese Etruscan," early 3rd cent. BC

Comb with sphinxes from Marsiliana, mid-7th cent. BC

The sarcophagus of Larthia Seianti from Chiusi, first half of the 2nd cent. BC

Two details of the "Sarcophagus of the Amazons" from Tarquinia, 375 BC

refined paintings with which it is adorned represent scenes of combat between Greeks and Amazons, in which it is possible to distinguish Achilles supporting the dying Amazon Penthesilea. Etruscan and Roman gold work is usually on show in the gallery of the wing that formerly housed the topographic section.

On the third floor collections of Greek figured pottery imported from Attica by the Etruscans are displayed in modern showcases, which have replaced the old glass cabinets. The undisputed masterpiece of this section is the famous *François Vase*, made by the potter Ergotimos and the vase painter Cleitias, who decorated it with superimposed friezes of mythological scenes. Dating from around 570 BC, the pot is painted with black figures and embellished with incised details. The technique was replaced (late 6th – early 5th cent. BC) by the contrasting red-figure style, in which the background of the vase was painted black, leaving the figures in red. Details were then added with the paintbrush, producing innovative effects of shading and foreshortening. This was the technique used by Myson, the "Berlin Painter," the "Cleophrades Painter" and others to realize the large vases in room V, the bowls in room VI and the large vases produced in Athens after the victories over the Persians that are on display in rooms VII and VIII. Room VIII also contains a number of "white-ground" vases made in the second half of the 5th cent. BC, using a technique in which the vase was first covered with a ground of white and cream and then the figures

painted in red with black outlines.

Also on temporary display on the third floor are Greek, Roman and Renaissance bronzes, the majority of which were once in the Medicean collections. They include the Medici-Riccardi *Horse's Head*, which belonged to Lorenzo the Magnificent, and the *Livorno Torso*, previously in the collection of Cosimo I. Both are in all likelihood Greek originals, the former Hellenistic, the second from the 5th cent. BC, and were to inspire a great deal of Renaissance sculpture, as the various works on show with them demonstrate. Roman sculpture is documented by the remains of an equestrian group found in the sandpits at Signa near Florence, and the two late Roman helmets with masks and skullcaps from Rapolano near Siena, reproducing youthful features in a classical style, are also of considerable interest. Alongside small

bronzes and metal oil lamps we find examples of noble portraiture (heads of Tiberius and Hadrian's favorite Antinous) and a group of four bronze heads fished from the waters of the Meloria in 1722: initially thought to be ancient, these are now considered 17th-century replicas of Roman works after Greek originals. (M.M.)

The *François Vase* from Fonte Rotella near Chiusi, 570 BC

Tazza attributed to the Lyandros Painter, second half of the 5th cent. BC

THE NORTHERN COAST
OF THE TYRRHENIAN SEA

In recent years the coastal region of Northwestern Tuscany has been subjected to archeological research that has underlined its importance and frequentation in ancient times. It is a vast area that slopes down from the Lunigiana and the Apuan Alps to the coast of Versilia and the sea, linked to Monte Pisano and, further inland, Lucca and the plain to the east. In the past the latter was connected to the great bed of the drained Lake of Bientina by a now vanished branch of the Serchio, called the Auser.

Prehistory

The presence of numerous mountainous areas has favored human settlement in caves and gorges since prehistoric times. Some of the most significant finds have been made at the Tecchia di Equi, in the vicinity of Equi Terme in Lunigiana, which has yielded stone artifacts from the Middle Paleolithic that are attributed to the "Mousterian" culture (named after the locality of Le Moustier in France) and document the presence of Neanderthals. Later frequented by populations of the Copper Age, this rock shelter connected to a cave is now open to the public, and part of the material found in it is on display in the Museo del Territorio dell'Alta Valle Aulella at Casola in Lunigiana.

The Garfagnana was also occupied in the Paleolithic, as the oldest materials in the Museo Archeologico at Castelnuovo Garfagnana demonstrate, although interesting finds

from the sandpits around Massaciuccoli Lake prove that it was not just the high ground that offered shelter to human beings at the time.

The occupation of these sites was far more extensive in the Copper and Bronze Ages. We know that in the Chalcolithic the populations of the zone deposited their dead in caves, sometimes burying them there immediately, but at others moving their bones to natural cavities in the rock after interring them elsewhere. An example of the former is the grave from the Grotta dell'Inferno at Vecchiano, now reconstructed in the Musei Civici of Viareggio, while the second case is represented by the Buca delle Fate, where human remains were ritually deposed. Among the finds typical of the Chalcolithic are precious triangular daggers made of copper and metal bracelets and axes, while the contemporary pottery can be classified into three types, with a scored surface, with overlapping scales and with applications in relief. In addition, there are some specimens with an engraved geometric decoration, typical of the "Bell-Beaker" culture.

A limited area between the valley of the Magra and the Apuan Alps saw the diffusion of a number of unusual sculptures from the early Metal Ages. Known as the "statue-stelae of Lunigiana," they only have a few parallels with other artifacts of the Alpine area and Europe

Opposite, two Copper-Age stelae of the "Malgrate" type from Lunigiana. Museo delle Statue Stele Lunigianesi, Pontremoli

Some Copper-Age stelae of the "Pontevecchio" type from Lunigiana. Museo delle Statue Stele Lunigianesi, Pontremoli

in general. The oldest examples, dating from the Copper Age (3400-2000 BC), have been divided into the "Pontevecchio" or A type and "Malgrate" or B type. The former has the characteristic appearance of a large slab of stone rounded at the top, with simple features of the human face reproduced in the upper part but no sign of a neck; the latter, in contrast, has a short and distinct neck, underneath a semicircular head. On both types arms and distinguishing attributes, such as weapons, are represented in bas-relief. While the function of these sculptures is not clear, it is possible that they were placed inside sacred precincts, not necessarily used as cemeteries. A third type (called "Reusa" or C), much closer to a rudimentary statue with exclusively male connotations, is believed to date from the Iron Age, as is suggested by the inscriptions in the Etruscan alphabet carved on some specimens. A wide range of these sculptures can be seen in the Museo delle Statue Stele Lunigianesi, housed in the picturesque Castello del Piagnaro at Pontremoli, while there are two more examples in the museum at Casola in Lunigiana.

Archeological investigations have identified the sites of numerous Bronze-Age settlements throughout the area, although some of them were only occupied seasonally, in connection with the practice of stockbreeding and thus transhumance. In addition to the well-known site of Romita di Asciano on the southern slopes of Monte Pisano, frequented until the Early Bronze Age, excavations have uncovered shelters in the area of Candalla, on the heights of Camaiore: the materials are on display at the museum in Viareggio. The widespread nature of finds from the most recent and final phase of the Bronze Age, very common in Garfagnana, Versilia and the area between Lucca and Pisa, indicates that the region was experiencing a spurt of growth in manufacturing as well as trade, closely connected with the presence of deposits of copper-bearing minerals. The exploitation of lacustrine resources around the former bed of Bientina Lake and along the course of the Auser River favored occupation of the area by human groups. Evidence for this comes from, among others, the finds made at Fossa Nera, in the commune of Porcari, where the characteristics of the metal and ceramic artifacts show strong ties with the western plain of Emilia.

Pisa

The ancient literary sources assign Pisa an origin in the remote past, recounting the legend of its foundation by a force of Greek veterans of the Trojan War. On the other hand, recent archeological research has identified the remains of a village of at least eight huts from the Late Bronze Age on Via di Gello. It was built on piles made from the trunks of elm trees in a setting of brackish lagoons.

The abandonment of this area at the end of the Bronze Age and the more or less contemporary existence of other settlements in the urban area of Pisa as well as at the mouth of the Arno seem to establish a direct link between the distribution of the villages and the instability of the water regime, but at the same time they demonstrate the marked preference for the location of settlements in piedmont areas and at the mouths of rivers on the coast. At the time the landscape was profoundly different from what we see today: the beaches were much shorter, the shoreline as far as Versilia was edged with lagoons and bodies of freshwater that constituted an easy berth for seafarers and useful source of fish and the rivers split at their mouths into various branches that could be navigated. The presence of materials from Sardinia – as well as objects influenced by the styles of what are now Northwestern Italy and France – in coastal sites reflects the scale on which maritime trade was conducted as far back as the beginning of the Iron Age.

In this context Pisa appears to have been a center of great importance from the 9th cent. BC onward, the period from which date several Villanovan tombs and traces of an inhabited

The tumulus
of Via San Jacopo in Pisa,
8th-7th cent. BC

A section of planking,
still being excavated,
of one of the Roman
vessels found at
San Rossore near Pisa

area within the limits of the modern city. As has already been pointed out, the original Pisan settlement was located in the vicinity of a lagoon separated from the sea by sandbanks, at the point where the northernmost branch of the Arno delta merged with the Auser. In all probability the community lay on a route of trade by land and river that led from Bologna over the Apennines to the area around Florence and then, by river, to Pisa. In the 8th century this route must have been joined by another, running from the region of Modena to the valleys of the Panaro and then along the Serchio to this port on the coast. Moreover, a number of bronze artifacts show that it was linked down the coast with Southern Etruria and the mouth of the Tiber. The discovery of fragments of pottery that may have been made at Tarquinia in the deepest archeological levels of Piazza del Duomo indicates that Pisa was a center for the importation and diffusion of Geometric-style ceramics from Southern Etruria to the northern coast and interior of Tuscany. In addition, this connection with the city in Latium has revived interest in the ancient literary sources, such as Cato, who attributed the foundation of Pisa to Tarchon, a legendary figure who is also said to have founded Tarquinia.

Other archeological researches in the Pisan area, on Via San Jacopo, have brought a large mound surrounded by stone slabs from the 8th-7th cent. BC to light in a Villanovan necropolis. Owing to the absence of human remains, it is thought likely to have been a cenotaph for a wealthy aristocrat. The area has been restored and opened to the public.

There is no doubt that at the end of the 7th century the city already controlled the territory stretching from Castiglioncello and the mouth of the Fine as far as Northern Versilia, and inland to the valley of the Serchio, the lower valley of the Arno and the middle valley of the Era. Its affluence fueled by flourishing handicrafts and agriculture (especially the production of wine, which was exported to France and Southern Etruria), Pisa reorganized its urban structure between the end of the 5th cent. BC and the beginning of the 4th, as the sanctuaries of Piazza Dante and Piazza del Duomo demonstrate. Further evidence of the city's development is provided by the remains of port facilities and the minting of its own silver currency. Becoming an ally of Rome as early as the 3rd cent. BC, Pisa was at the center of the fighting with the Ligurians, who from that time on stepped up their pressure on both the coastal area and the lands to the north of the lower course of the Arno. From its Roman period – between 41 and 33 BC it was named Colonia Opsequens Iulia – remain the baths of Porta a Lucca, dating from the 1st cent. AD (and called "The Baths of Nero"), and some sculptures in the Museo dell'Opera del Duomo and Camposanto.

In December 1998, in the course of work on the construction of the operations headquarters of the State Railroads at the station of San Rossore, an exceptional archeological discovery was made: the remains of the urban harbor of the Etruscan and Roman city were brought to light and, with them, the wrecks of at least 28 vessels. The vestiges of the port facilities of the Etruscan city have been identified in the southernmost part of the excavated area. Subsequently silted up, they consisted of a palisade that acted as a breakwater along which ran a quay built of large blocks of stone. Almost 2 m wide and 16 long, it was connected to a quadrangular structure that jutted outward.

Some of the finds associated with these structures (*impasto* pots, a cup with a graffito inscription in Etruscan, black-glaze vases, an Etruscan column krater) date from as early as the 5th cent. BC. But the most exciting discovery was that of 28 boats, together with their cargoes and stores, still in an excellent state of preservation thanks to the wet and anaerobic soil that has prevented deterioration of the timbers and organic substances. The hulls of three cargo boats, three craft for river navigation, an oared ship and two more large vessels whose use has still to be determined are more or less intact, while other hulls are incomplete and damaged. The dates of the ships cover a long lapse of time, extending from the 3rd cent. BC to the 5th AD, and they must have sunk in the harbor for a variety of motives, ranging from bad weather to human action.

The recovery of the material is still underway, as is its restoration, which is going to take a fairly long time. However, some of the objects have already been put on show at temporary exhibitions held in the Arsenali dei Cavalieri di Santo Stefano.

Versilia and the Lucca Region

The port of Pisa was not the only one established by the Etruscans on the coast. One of the more significant of those identified by excavations must have been the port at San Rocchino, in the vicinity of Massarosa, whose faint traces on the ground have now faded. Here, not far from a source of fresh water, were uncovered some remains from the Early Iron Age where a complex work of drainage of the land and containment of the water in the lagoon was carried out at the end of the 7th cent. BC. Palings were erected as breakwaters and dikes constructed out of heaps of fascines and wood arranged to form caissons of regular shape. In the remains of the dwellings built on top of these substructures have been found *bucchero*, colorless and *impasto* pots that show close parallels with objects excavated in Pisa, the countryside around Volterra and Populonia. Fragments of black- and red-figure vases imported from Greece as well as locally produced pottery date from the end of the 6th and the 5th century. The most significant pieces from this site are now on display in the archeological section of the Museo di Villa Guinigi in Lucca, while other objects can be seen at the Archeological Museum of Viareggio.

Various finds made in Versilia are connected with the presence of Etruscans, bearing witness to the existence of trade links with the north. These led to the foundation of small settlements at the mouth of the Magra and in the gulf of La Spezia, as well as a probable concurrent withdrawal on the part of the Ligurians, whose cemeteries at Chiavari, Rapallo and the Baccatoio appear to have been aban-

Bowl and dipper from Chiarone di Capannori, late 7th cent. BC. Museo Nazionale di Villa Guinigi, Lucca

Small votive bronzes representing women from Buca di Castelvenere, 450-420 BC. Museo Nazionale di Villa Guinigi, Lucca

Two faces of the Attic *kelebe* attributed to the Painter of the Hog from Rio Ralletta near Capannori, *circa* 470 BC. Museo Nazionale di Villa Guinigi, Lucca

doned at the beginning of the 6th cent. BC.

Other vestiges from the period are present further inland, in Garfagnana, along the valley of the Serchio and around the ancient Lake of Bientina: the materials from these sites are displayed in the archeological museums of Castelnuovo Garfagnana (Etruscan and Ligurian artifacts dating from between the 6th and 2nd cent. BC), Barga (grave goods from the Ligurian tombs of Castelvecchio Pascoli and Val di Vaiana), and Pietrasanta (funeral symbols in the form of clubs, characteristic of the Etruscan phase in Versilia.

The Villanovan, Orientalizing and Archaic materials from the settlement at Chiarone di Capannori have gone to the Museo di Villa Guinigi in Lucca, along with some of the finds from Buca di Castelvenere. Above all, however, the museum houses elegant gold work and the fine Attic red-figure krater with Theseus, the work of the "Painter of the Pig," that was used as a cinerary urn for an Etruscan grave at Rio Ralletta di Capannori; the trove of silver coins from the beginning of the 3rd cent. BC from Romito di Pozzuolo; the contemporary Ligurian case tombs from Vado di Camaiore, evidence for the advance of the Ligurians in this period; and the case tomb from Pulica in Lunigiana (3rd cent. BC), which contained, in addition to a cinerary vase and pottery, a number of fine examples of weaponry, including a sword, a spear and a rare bronze helmet with large horns of sheet metal.

It would be left to the Roman army to deal with the Ligurians, although they encountered very stiff resistance that lasted, through various campaigns, until 180 BC, when the Ligurian defeat was followed by the deportation of 40 000 men to the Samnium. This cleared the way for the foundation of the colonies of Lucca and Luni in 177 BC.

Thus the Museo di Villa Guinigi covers the entire archeological history of Lucca, which stretches all the way back to the Etruscan era as the finds made on Via Squaglia attest. Dating from the late 7th-early 6th cent. BC, these come from a family burial ground made up of about a

dozen graves containing cremated bodies, perhaps connected with the nearby settlement on Via Nottolini, where fragments of *bucchero* and other ware have been uncovered. A collection of Roman and Longobard materials completes the documentation of the city's history, of which further evidence is provided by the remains of the amphitheater, visible in Piazza dell'Anfiteatro, and of buildings from the Roman period under the church of Santi Giovanni e Reparata.

Other significant traces of the Etruscans have been found at Fossa Nera, near Porcari in the Luccan plain, where a rural settlement with dwellings, grain stores and middens was founded in the years spanning the 6th and 5th cent. BC, in an area that had been occupied in the Bronze Age and then abandoned due to the overflow of the Auser. After suffering damage from one inundation, the village was destroyed by another flood that affected the whole of the Bientina marsh and transformed the life and economy of the entire region, driving the Etruscans out of the area until the 3rd cent. BC. The site at Fossa Nera was reoccupied around 150 BC, in the Roman era, by a later Republican house surrounded by a large number of small farms and buildings that have been identified in recent excavations. Vestiges of these phases can be seen in the permanent archeological exhibitions at Porcari and Capannori, as well as in the Museo Etrusco Comunale of Bientina, located near what had been a large lake in the Middle Ages, but which was drained in the 19th century.

Remains of the Roman villa of the Venulei near Massaciuccoli Lake, 1st cent. AD

The Settlements of the Period of Roman Colonization

The archeological area of Massaciuccoli, facing onto the lake of the same name, also refers to the Roman era. Open to the public, it contains the remains of a large villa built on terraces at the beginning of the 1st cent. AD for the Pisan family of the Venulei, wealthy manufacturers of bricks. While the upper part of the ancient complex is now occupied by the parish church of San Lorenzo, the lower terraces with *nymphaea*, pools, baths and a *triclinium* with an exedra can still be seen; excavations are still being carried out there.

Further north, at the locality of Capezzano Pianore, a Roman farm with equipment for the production of oil has been brought to light. It is located on the slopes of the first coastal hills, significantly in an area that would later be traversed by the Via Francigena. A double press has been identified inside the building, along with basins for settling the oil in the vicinity of the area set aside for storage of the products. The materials found on the site are displayed in the Museo Civico Archeologico of Camaiore, while there are plans to open the site of the villa to the public.

The oldest marble quarries in the Apuan Alps, dating from the 1st cent. BC, were of great importance in the Roman era. Traces of them have been identified through excavation in the environs of Colonnata, Torano and Miseglia. The Museo Civico del Marmo in Carrara houses artifacts, coins and religious statues, as well as semifinished materials (columns, capitals, bases) ready to be shipped, mainly from Luni, to the places where they would be given their final touches. Also on display in the museum in Carrara are sections of the surface of ancient quarries, called "slices," that show the marks left by the Roman quarrymen. Other contemporary finds can be seen at the Accademia di Belle Arti in Carrara, which can be visited in conjunction with the Archeological Museum and the excavated area of the ancient city of Luni in Liguria, in the vicinity of Sarzana. Of this city, a colony and port founded by the Romans (177 BC), on the site of an earlier settlement dating from the end of the 3rd cent. BC, a large part of the built-up area and the road system has been preserved, along with remains of the walls, the forum with the *Capitolium*, the theater, the northern temple and the amphitheater outside the Eastern gate. (M.M.)

THE ETRUSCANS OF THE PO VALLEY

The cultural aspects of that part of the Po Valley occupied by the Etruscans are just as old as those of areas in Etruria proper. In fact the name ("Villanovan") given to the Etruscan culture of the Early Iron Age comes from a place in Emilia near Bologna, Villanova, where the first evidence of this cultural *stratum* was brought to light. Thus several areas of Romagna and Emilia as far as the Po show a substantial identity with the territories to the south of the Apennines, a barrier that in reality had been traversed since prehistoric times by numerous passes linking Emilia with the Pistoia region and the countryside around Florence, and Romagna with the Mugello and the Val di Sieve.

However, features of the Villanovan culture lasted in the Po Valley until sometime round the middle of the 6th cent. BC, i.e. well beyond the chronological limits usually assigned to them in Etruria proper, with a persistence of traditional sociocultural schemes and patterns of settlement that hindered the formation of true cities. In reality we know that certain evolutionary processes induced by manufacturing, commercial and craft activities rather than agricultural ones first emerged in Southern Etruria and then, through expansion, spread northward and eastward, consistently with the tenacity of certain cultural traditions and the absence of close contacts with other peoples of the Mediterranean.

Bologna

The capital of Emilia, located at the heart of a territory inhabited since prehistoric times, was occupied in the 9th cent. BC by peoples of Villanovan culture from a number of nearby settlements whose vestiges and cemeteries have been identified: some of the most important were those of Benacci-Caprara, Benacci, Certosa, Arnoaldi and De Luca. The evolution of the local Villanovan culture started out from villages made up of oval or angular huts – like the one engraved on stele 793 from San Vitale – and well tombs containing cremated remains and scanty, not very differentiated grave goods, reflecting the fairly uniform character of the society of the time. In the first half of the 8th cent. BC the areas of settlement in the Bologna region shifted to the west, in connection with the courses of two rivers, and the contents of tombs began to grow richer, attaining conspicuous levels between the second half of the 8th century and the first half of the

7th, when metal articles became plentiful and showed the influence of models from Vetulonia and Tarquinia. The frequent presence of weapons of offense (those of defense being more perishable) in the tombs of men is a sign of the social and economic rise of warriors, especially mounted ones, of which the famous Benacci *askos* constitutes the prime example.

Opposite, the "Benacci Askos" from Tomb 525 of the Benacci burial ground in Bologna, second half of the 8th cent. BC. Museo Civico Archeologico, Bologna

The "Zannoni Stone" from Bologna, late 7th cent. BC. Museo Civico Archeologico, Bologna

The "Malvasia-Tortorelli Stone" from Via Santo Stefano in Bologna, mid-7th cent. BC. Museo Civico Archeologico, Bologna

Further evidence for the flourishing state of the various settlements in the Bologna area is provided by the store of bronzes found at San Francesco, which originally consisted of a hut housing a partially buried large clay *dolium* containing about 15 000 objects made of bronze and just three of iron. They are now on display at Bologna's Museo Civico Archeologico. People were buried in individual graves, increasingly often inhumations, and the inscriptions, in the Etruscan language, show that the strong clans of families – *gentes* – already present in Southern Etruria were not yet widespread. Nonetheless, there was no lack of cultural and artistic influences, as is demonstrated by the more and more common presence of ornamentation with figures of men, animals and plants on vessels, alongside traditional geometric motifs.

Verucchio

The settlement of Verucchio, located on an inaccessible hill in the hinterland, where the middle valley of the Marecchia joins up with the Rimini plain, also dates from the period between the 9th and 7th cent. BC. It was probably the principal Etruscan center of Villanovan culture in Romagna. While in the 9th century the Villanovan presence in the Bolognese area was closely connected with communities in Northern Etruria located between the Arno and the Ombrone, that of Romagna and the Marche (Fermo) should be linked with the peoples living in Etruria to the north of the Tiber, in particular at Tarquinii and Veii. Up to the middle of the 6th cent. BC the local culture was characterized by evolutionary forms of the Villanovan that are highly distinctive and indicative of great wealth. While traces of the inhabited areas have been found in the form of bases of huts, wells and pottery kilns, it is the tombs that have yielded really spectacular contents. Some of them have even been spared the attentions of looters and the effects of en-

vironmental factors. In fact the dampness of the ground and the infiltration of water have preserved materials like cloth, wood, hide, fleece, wicker and food, by protecting them from the action of bacteria. The objects found in Lippi Tomb 85 included wooden ones like a decorated throne with a high back, a footrest and three round, three-legged tables. There was also a wickerwork helmet reinforced with bronze studs and traces of the linen tunic that had been used to cover the ossuary. Tomb 89, structurally similar, also contained a wooden throne with carvings of scenes from daily life and ceremonial parades. In addition to numerous objects in bronze, including shields made of sheets of the metal, there was a helmet that still had part of its double crest of horsehair and an ax with its original wooden handle. These materials are on display at the Museo Civico Archeologico of Verucchio, where the contents of a shaft that had been used to deposit votive material up until the first half of the 4th cent. BC can also be seen.

The Etruscanization of the Po Valley and Marzabotto

Bronze statuette of man praying from the votive deposit of Monte Acuto Ragazza at Grizzana near Bologna, 480-460 BC. Museo Civico Archeologico, Bologna

Two faces of the "Certosa Situla" from Tomb 68 of the burial ground of the Certosa in Bologna, late 6th cent. BC. Museo Civico Archeologico, Bologna

In the middle of the 6th cent. BC part of the Po Valley underwent processes of transformation that coincided with the migration of people from several cities in Etruria, above all Clusium (Chiusi). These changes had numerous concomitant causes, such as the Etruscan withdrawal from Campania, the growing conflict between the fleets operating in the Tyrrhenian Sea and the Greek interest in Central European markets, prompting them to develop trade routes through the Adriatic to reach them. As a consequence, the search for new commercial outlets and new lands to meet the needs of a growing population led to the introduction of typically "Etruscan" peoples and aspects of material culture into the Villanovan tradition of the Po Valley.

It was only at this moment that Felsina (Bologna), acquired an urban character it had not previously had, extending between the watercourses of the Aposa and Ravone. Yet some traditions were preserved: the cemeteries maintained continuity with the preceding period, and preference was still shown for individual burials in well tombs, although such new

fashions as the use of imported Attic kraters and vases as cinerary urns were accepted. The introduction of the scheme of the organization of society into *gentes* is documented by epigraphs, and an effective representation of the new social structure is provided by the reliefs on the *situla* from the necropolis of the Certosa in Bologna, representing scenes of aristocratic life and an army made up of the middle class. While the costumes of the nobility seem to be influenced by Oriental and Greek as well as Central European fashions, the various corps of the army appear to come from an only moderately prosperous stratum of the population. These lower classes are diversified in their armament, and therefore in their wealth. Hence in some areas of Etruria the military units only partly followed the Greek model of the hoplite phalanx, characterized by the uniformity of its components.

The fortune of cities like Bologna rose in the 5th cent. BC, when the loss of Etruscan naval supremacy, after the defeat at Cumae, made the centers on the roads uniting Etruria with the new markets on the Adriatic coast

even more important. On one of these routes,
to the south of Bologna, arose Marzabotto
which, although inhabited since the middle of
the 6th cent. BC, was then "founded" at the
beginning of the 5th with a carefully drawn-up
and modular colonial plan, matching that of
the settlement of Gonfienti in the Prato region.
Thus a city was laid out in a grid on a plateau
delimited by a bend in the Reno, its alignment
determined by the temples of the acropolis
(facing south for religious reasons, and located
on the northern *decumanus*), with a paved *cardo* and three 15-m-wide *decumani*. While the
characteristics of this settlement (predating
the principles laid down by Hippodamus of
Miletus, the Greek theorist of regularized city
planning) are chiefly due to religious requirements, something typical of Etruscan society,
they have evident technical, practical and social applications, coinciding in part with the
later political and philosophical ideas of Hippodamus, connected with the emergence of
democracy in Athens.

The *insulae*, i.e. the blocks, of Marzabotto
were made up of large houses built of unfired
brick on a foundation of stones, usually with
just one story and workshops and stores facing
onto the street. The central entrance led into
the courtyard in the *impluvium* (whose introduction is attributed by the literature to the
Etruscans), onto which opened the rooms. Special blocks were devoted to manufacturing activities, such as potteries and metal workshops. A tour of the entire archeological complex allows the visitor to appreciate the size of
the city, while the local museum recounts the
history of the settlement, up until its sudden
abandonment (early 4th cent. BC) as a result of
the occupation of the area by Celtic populations between the middle of the 4th cent. BC
and the second half of the 3rd.

Spina, Adria and the Other Centers

The Greek or in any case non-Etruscan origin of Spina, founded at the mouth of a branch of the Po River, is mentioned in many ancient literary sources. However, Etruscans and Greeks were both present from the mid-6th cent. BC onward, when Spina became a great *emporion* where huge amounts of pottery arrived from Attica, later recovered from tombs and displayed at the Museo Archeologico Nazionale in Ferrara.

The built-up area was divided into several blocks, the largest of which covered 6 hectares. The sides exposed to the sea were protected by dikes of pilework, while the blocks – made up of houses with walls of wooden planks or lathwork covered with clay – were separated by a grid of streets and canals. The tombs, found in the areas of Valle Pega and Valle Trebba, were usually simple pits in the ground holding wooden chests.

In the 5th century, with the establishment of Syracusan dominance over the Tyrrhenian, Spina's economy was given a new boost as it took on the role of a clearing center for the products of its own hinterland and of Central Europe (grain, agricultural produce, timber, metals, amber) on their way to the Greek world. And it was from Hellas, moving in the opposite direction, that all kinds of pottery arrived for decades, but internal strife in Greece and Syracusan action in the Adriatic reduced the level of such commerce until it vanished altogether around 325 BC. After a period of relations with the Volterra region, the presence of the Gauls led to the decline of Spina in the middle of the 3rd cent. BC.

The history of Adria, situated between the Po and the Adige and linked to the sea by a navigable river branch, was similar. Inhabited since the 6th century, and perhaps home to a colony of Greeks, it was eclipsed around the middle of the 5th century by the rise of Spina. In addition to parts of the built-up area, here too formed of wooden houses, various necropolises have been identified. The materials from them are now in the local museum.

The Etruscan colonization of the Po Valley did not solely give rise to urban centers located on trade routes, but also produced a network of scattered farms, as in the case of the territory between the Secchia and the Cerca, in the Modena region. Here, at Baggiovara, the site of Case Vandelli has been excavated: the settlement was active in the 5th cent. BC and then abandoned at the beginning of the next.

The Celtic presence, already documented in the cisalpine area in the 7th-6th cent. BC, and initially lucrative for the increase in trade that it brought, ended up exercising growing military pressure as those populations were attracted by the prosperity of the Etruscan centers in the Po Valley and the fertile lands in the area. In rapid progression the majority of the settlements were abandoned by the Etruscans, who withdrew to the line of demarcation between the different spheres of influence along the ridge of the Apennines. However, the friction was also accompanied by trade, as is still documented in the 4th century at Mantua, the city that according to Virgil was founded by the Etruscan Ocnus and that in the 5th century became a fundamental junction on the routes leading to the Rhine and the Moselle. (M.M.)

End of candlestick with crotal player from Tomb 128 of the necropolis of Valle Trebba at Spina, first-second quarter of the 5th cent. BC. Museo Archeologico, Ferrara

Essential Bibliography

General Works

J. Heurgon, *Daily Life of the Etruscans*, London 1964

R. Bloch, *The Etruscans*, London 1958; repr. 1965

L. Banti, *Il mondo degli Etruschi*, Rome 1969

R. Bianchi Bandinelli and A. Giuliano, *Etruschi e italici prima del dominio di Roma*, Milan 1973

M. Cristofani, *L'arte degli Etruschi. Produzione e consumo*, Turin 1978

T.W. Potter, *The Changing Landscape of South Etruria*, New York 1979

M. Torelli, *Storia degli Etruschi*, Rome-Bari 1981

M. Pallottino, *Etruscologia*, Milan 1984 (7th ed.)

G. Camporeale and G. Morolli (eds.), *Gli Etruschi mille anni di civiltà*, Florence 1985

M. Cristofani (ed.), *Gli Etruschi. Una nuova immagine*, Florence 1985

M. Torelli, *L'arte degli Etruschi*, Rome-Bari 1985

G. Pugliese Carratelli (ed.) *Rasenna*, Milan 1986

M. Torelli, *La società etrusca*, Rome 1987

G. Bartoloni, *La cultura villanoviana*, Rome 1989

M. Cristofani, *Gli Etruschi del Mare*, Milan 1989

A.M. Bietti Sestieri, *Protostoria*, Rome 1996

Toscana etrusca e romana, Milan 2002

G. Bartoloni, *Le società dell'Italia primitiva*, Rome 2003

G. Camporeale, *Gli Etruschi. Storia e civiltà*, Turin 2004 (2nd ed.)

Exhibition Catalogues

M. Cristofani (ed.), *Civiltà degli Etruschi*, Milan 1985

Gli Etruschi e l'Europa, Milan 1992

Principi etruschi tra Mediterraneo ed Europa, Venice 2000

M. Torelli (ed.), *Gli Etruschi*, Milan 2000

G.C. Cianferoni (ed.), *The World of the Etruscans*, Shanghai 2003

G.C. Cianferoni (ed.), *Treasures from Tuscany – The Etruscan Legacy*, Edinburgh 2004

The illustrations in this volume have been supplied by the
SCALA PICTURE LIBRARY,
the largest source of color transparencies and digital images
of the visual arts in the world.
The over 60,000 subjects visible at the site
www.scalarchives.it

can be accessed through computerized procedures
that permit easy and rapid picture searches of any complexity.

e-mail: archivio@scalagroup.com

The images from the SCALA Picture Library reproducing cultural assets
that belong to the Italian State are published with the permission
of the Ministry for Cultural Heritage and Activities.

Texts: Maurizio Martinelli (M.M.) and Giulio Paolucci (G.P.)

Graphic design: Matilde Contri
Translation: Huw Evans

Photographs: Archivio Fotografico SCALA Group (S. Lampredi)
except pp. 19, 46a, 155b, 183a (British Museum, HIP/SCALA);
pp. 199b, 220, 221 (M. Martinelli); p. 211 (Soprintendenza
per i Beni Archeologici della Toscana)

Printed by: Industria Grafica Bieffe, Recanati (MC), 2023